The Art of
PENNSYLVANIA DUTCH COOKING

Author's Previous Books

DUTCH COOKBOOK, VOLUME II

EDNA EBY HELLER'S DUTCH COOKBOOK

A PINCH OF THIS AND A HANDFUL OF THAT

A PINCH OF THIS AND A HANDFUL OF THAT, VOLUME II

The Art of
PENNSYLVANIA
DUTCH COOKING

Edna Eby Heller

ILLUSTRATED BY RAY CRUZ

GALAHAD BOOKS • NEW YORK CITY

Dedicated to Mother,
whose courage has been
my inspiration

Preface

THE purpose of this book is to bring Pennsylvania Dutch cooking right into your kitchen, if you please. These recipes, or receipts, as our mothers called them, have been passed from generation to generation by word of mouth, with each housewife learning the art of cookery by experience. With the creative touch of an artist she adds water to flour and shortening until the pastry "feels just right," or mixes a batter until it "looks just right." When recipes are written for a friend or relative, not all measurements of ingredients are given, and frequently the only directions included are: "sugar to sweeten and flour to stiffen."

I have listened and watched, then measured and tested, so that this regional cookery could be made practical for the present generation of cookbook cooks. Consequently, all of the recipes in the book are given in standardized measurements.

The recipes have been gathered from various counties, for each section of the Pennsylvania Dutch territory seems to have a few of its own likes and dislikes. Carbon and Lehigh counties prefer their own style of serving Schnitz un Knepp* with milk, while the folks of other counties serve it with ham. Berks County cooks make Potpie* light with baking powder, but York County folks like it heavy. The saffron herb is treasured in Lancaster, but despised in Kutztown. However, in contrast to those differences, Shoo-Fly Pie* is served throughout the whole Pennsylvania Dutch area.

It is my sincere hope that this volume will bring enjoyment and good eating to many households. To those who have shared with me their hand-written receipt books or kindly given me family recipes, and to the editors of *Pennsylvania Folklife* for kind permission to reprint recipes appearing in my articles, I shall be forever grateful.

EDNA EBY HELLER

Contents

Recipes that are indicated in the text by an asterisk * can be found by referring to the Index.

Introduction

WHO ARE THE PENNSYLVANIA DUTCH?

Among the hills of eastern Pennsylvania, tourists and antique collectors have discovered the treasures of the Pennsylvania Dutch. They are fascinated by kitchen chairs that are decorated with colorful flowers and scrolls and by designs, called hex signs, painted on barns "just for pretty." The collectors beg and barter for butter molds, cookie cutters, glassware, pottery, and punched tinware that has been decorated with hearts and tulips.

Who are these Pennsylvania Dutch? They are Pennsylvanians or descendants of Pennsylvanians, but they are not really Dutch.

The name Pennsylvania Dutch was given to the early settlers on
Penn's land by their neighbors, because they left Europe from
Holland. The misnomer has never been effectively erased. Penn-
sylvania German would be a more accurate name.

Probably another reason that the misnomer stayed with us
is because of the language. Even though most of the Pennsylvania Dutch are of German or Swiss extraction, the language
spoken (used mostly by the older generation today) is a dialect
with many words coined here in the New World. The fact
that the language was not pure German would have been good
reason not to use the name Pennsylvania German.

The first settlers came to Pennsylvania in 1683. The greatest
number of them came from the European Palatinate—the
Rhine Valley in Germany. The fact that the majority of im-
migrants were farmers determined their pattern of settlement.
They landed at Philadelphia and followed the Susquehanna and
Schuylkill rivers, settling wherever they found black walnut
trees and limestone soil. This, they knew would be fertile land.
With these farmers came artists, weavers, potters, doctors, stu-
dents, and teachers. Because they had a self-sufficient community, they mingled very little with neighboring settlers. However, in time, they moved into the Northwest Territory, the
South, and the Midwest to the extent that there are now thousands of displaced Pennsylvania Dutch throughout the United
States.

In Pennsylvania Dutch land, there were, and still are, many
religious sects. Among the early settlers were Lutherans, Reformed, Moravians, Seventh-Day Baptists, Schwenkfelders, Men-
nonites, Dunkards, and the Amish. Members of the last three
of these sects are called "Plain People" because their way of
life is as plain and simple as their mode of dress and method
of worship. The emphasis is on simplicity. "Plain People" strive
to follow St. Paul's instructions to separate themselves from
the things of the world.

The Amish sect are the plainest of the "Plain People." They
shun modern conveniences such as telephones, radios, television,

and even electricity. Their horse and buggy transportation completely fascinates twentieth-century tourists. Amish men can also be recognized by their beards and wide-brimmed hats; the women and children by their black aprons and capes.

The majority of settlers in eastern Pennsylvania were members of the Lutheran and Reformed churches. By way of contrast, these "non-Plain" people were called "Church People." Of these, the minority groups were the Seventh-Day Baptists and the Schwenkfelders. Of greater number were the Moravians. They brought an exuberant spirit of culture which prompted them to be among the early founders of secondary schools, colleges, and musical organizations.

Like the early settlers, the twentieth-century Pennsylvania Dutch are Christians who cherish their religion above everything else. They are an industrious folk who demonstrate their belief that the virtues of thrift and cleanliness rank next to godliness.

DAY-BY-DAY COOKERY

During the early years of settlement, supplies were scanty and the cooking was extremely simple. Turning the virgin forests of eastern Pennsylvania into the garden spot of America, as it is known today, was an achievement that took time. Our ancestors were, of necessity, a thrifty people who found ingenious ways to use the food that was on hand.

In spite of their thrifty ways, one extravagance that Pennsylvania Dutch cooks enjoyed was the free use of butter. They still feel that nothing can take the place of true butter flavor and so they continue to use it lavishly. The diet is heavy and full of starch, but no one seems to care. They do not bother to count calories. Some say, "Neither a fat wife nor a full barn ever did any man harm!" So there are dumplings galore and meat with potatoes three times a day. Even pie for breakfast is not unusual.

The breakfast served on the farm is quite a meal. Corn meal

mush with meat pudding or scrapple are traditional breakfast dishes. Potatoes are served with either fried ham, bacon, dried beef gravy, or sausage. There is fruit, perhaps several fruits, and cereal. In addition, there may be corn fritters or fruit fritters that might be filled with cherries, apples, or elderberries. Finally, "to top off on"—either crumb cakes, shoo-fly pies, or cookies.

About nine in the morning the farmer is ready for his mid-morning lunch. It used to be customary for the children to carry this to the fields in a basket and jug; today it is done only at harvest time. The lunch might be either freshly made Funnel Cakes,* Snavely Sticks,* doughnuts, or cookies. In the jug there is Ginger Water,* or perhaps Vinegar Punch*—simple beverages, yet to the farmer they are the world's best thirst-quenchers.

The dinner at noontime is the biggest meal of the day. Tables are laden with meat, potatoes, noodles or dumplings, several vegetables, homemade bread, many sweets and sours, a pudding or two, fruits, and pie.

The evening meal, called supper, is much lighter than dinner. Most likely there will be slices of cold beef or ham, fried potatoes, and one of the Pennsylvania Dutch cheeses. The most common of these is spread on top of apple-butter bread. In the Pennsylvania Dutch dialect we call it *lottwaerrick un schmierkase* (apple butter and cottage cheese), and everyone puts a layer of each on butter bread. Egg Cheese,* made in heart-shaped punched-tin molds, is another homemade cheese that is often on the supper table. Sharper cheeses are cup cheese and ball cheese. Supper is also the meal for soups, corn pone, apple dumplings, steamed puddings, and shortcakes, served as the main part of the supper meal. The dessert may be pie or cake, or perhaps both. Bread and coffee are included with every meal.

What about salads? They are a healthy addition to any diet, but the Pennsylvania Dutch have few. The salad section of a Pennsylvania Dutch cookbook is a small one. Served as a side dish and never as a separate course, salads are usually simple—just a dressing poured over greens, either lettuce, endive, cabbage, or dandelion. A hot Bacon Dressing* served on dandelion or leaf lettuce in the spring, or endive in the fall, is a favorite. Almost as popular is the sweet-sour vinegar dressing poured over cabbage slaw. Other sours served at the same meal will be pickled items such as watermelon rind (Pickled Watermelon*), Bread-and-Butter Pickles,* and Red Beet Eggs.* Jams, jellies, and canned fruits are the balancing sweets.

Much has been written about the "seven sweets and seven sours" of the Pennsylvania Dutch. This terminology, however, is actually a myth, for no housewife bothers to count the number of sweets and sours she puts on her table. It might just as likely be eight sweets and six sours, or four and four. There are always enough to make an interesting count but you shouldn't expect precisely seven.

Next to his sweets and sours, the Pennsylvania Dutchman enjoys his pie. Quite often we have pie three times a day, for breakfast, dinner, and supper. We eat cake pies, fruit pies, molasses pies, custard pies, and milk pies. Even vinegar pies! Shoo-Fly Pie* is the one that has brought the greatest renown to Pennsylvania Dutch foods. Long live its fame! Should there still be a mortal who would ask, "What is a shoo-fly pie?", the answer is simple. A molasses cake that is baked in a pie shell—that is a shoo-fly.

The simplicity of life which our forefathers sought to maintain influenced their cooking and kept their food tastes in the classification of simple cookery. Few herbs are used and foods are not highly seasoned. Near every kitchen is a bed of parsley and near it there may be chives, thyme, sweet marjoram, summer savory, saffron, and dill. Our grandmothers had coriander, caraway, and anise too. Along fences grow herbs to brew: mint, balsam, horehound, pennyroyal, and the medicinal boneset. As children, we were given that bitter boneset tea to cure stomach illnesses. Since then I've been told that we would have only needed to rub our hands over the leaves of a growing boneset plant!

The art of herb seasoning presents no problem to our women. Their general intuition in matters of cooking serves them well. Chives are used in soups, salads, and fried potatoes; thyme in soups (and for a spring tonic); sweet marjoram with pork, potato soup, and coleslaw. Summer savory belongs to green beans, just as dill belongs to pickles, and coriander to sausage.

COOKERY FOLKLORE

The common expression, "He is as Dutch as sauerkraut" shows the prominence of sauerkraut in this regional cookery. In fact, the year is begun with sauerkraut. It is a New Year's Day custom that dates back to Colonial times. We eat sauerkraut on the first day of January for health and good luck. This is a must! Although it is generally boiled with pork, the way it is served is not important.

The day before Ash Wednesday is a most significant day for the Pennsylvania Dutch menu. Shrove Tuesday is known as Fasnacht Day (night before the fast). It shows a trace of the European pre-Christian influence of the feast day celebrations for the advent of spring and to the spring goddess, Ostara. In Germany, along the Rhine, yeast doughnuts are still made for Shrove Tuesday. Like theirs, ours are usually rectangular with a slit cut in the center. However, some people prefer the round *fasnacht* because they particularly enjoy the "holes" (cut-out centers), which are also fried.

The folklorist enjoys Fasnacht Day as much as the children do. For some unexplainable reason the last one out of bed on Fasnacht Day is called either "lazy fasnacht," or "old cluck" and for breakfast gets only one fasnacht, quite likely a misshapen one. The fat used in frying the fasnachts is thought to have magic powers. If used to grease the garden spade and the plowing discs, good harvesting is sure to follow!

On Thursday of Holy Week the Pennsylvania Dutchman says he must take thought of his health. To him, eating greens on this day is an imperative requisite to good health. The lowly dandelion is the salad green most often used on this particular Thursday. Old and young alike go out into the meadows and gather the very young stalks. They are served with a boiled salad dressing made with bacon and bacon fat.

The spring months are exciting for the Pennsylvania Dutch housewife. After she finishes her meticulous house cleaning, her attention is focused on gardening. Even the town dwellers have gardens, which the housewife plants and constantly weeds. With eager anticipation she orders seeds, plans the garden, and plants her seeds in straight, straight rows. For planting she consults the Farmer's Almanac. It tells her when to plant, weed, and harvest. She knows that red beets and other plants with edible roots must be planted in the "down going" of the moon, but peas and beans are planted in the "up going."

HARVEST COOKERY

Fortunately, the tourists can enjoy the harvest too. They can tour the markets as well as the restaurants. Farm women have established marketing businesses selling their own poultry and garden vegetables. Their stands in the city Farmers' Markets are absolutely beautiful with produce that is irresistible. Carefully stacked and regularly sprayed with water from a little bulb sprayer to keep them fresh, the fruits and vegetables are the prettiest of their kind. Market visitors say they have never seen produce more beautiful than in Pennsylvania Dutch markets.

The long canning season begins when the rhubarb is turning pink in May, and lasts until late September when the last of the garden relish is canned. The canning of apples and mincemeat sometimes extends the season even further. Since freezing methods have been adopted, the volume of canning has decreased, but most housewives still can several hundred quarts per year. It is the drying of vegetables and fruits that is rapidly being replaced by the freezing process. The women who once dried pounds and pounds of beans, corn, apples, and peaches now have only a few bags of dried foods hanging from the attic rafters.

Three common processes are used for drying. In the kitchen, the fruits and vegetables are dried in slow ovens or spread on a drying pan over boiling water on the top of the stove. On very hot days, large quantities are dried outside in the sun. There are also a few "dry houses" still in use. They are unique buildings, about five feet square and six feet high, just big enough to house an old-fashioned wood stove. Drawer-like trays are built into the walls so that they can be filled from the outside. Using a "dry house," fruits and vegetables can be dried by the bushel.

In the past generations the apple harvest brought about the social event of the season: "schnitzing parties." Young and old gathered to peel and slice apples, an occasion even more festive than the ladies' quilting parties. In the dialect, *schnitz* means "slice," and is commonly used in reference to apple slices. At "schnitzing" parties, bushels of apples were cut for cider-making and apple butter-boiling.

HOLIDAY COOKERY

The religious celebration of Christmas is a festive occasion for every Pennsylvania Dutch family, but in the homes of Bethlehem, Pennsylvania, the holiday is observed with more elaborate decorations than elsewhere. It is a city predominately inhabited by Moravians who have continued their old-world customs throughout all these years. In the homes, the birth of the Christ child is depicted with a *putz,* the Pennsylvania Dutch manger scene. Weeks before Christmas each year the family begins to gather evergreens, tree stumps, and moss— enough to build a room-size display in the dining room or parlor.

In the hollows of the tree stumps the various scenes of the Christmas story are depicted: the Annunciation, the shepherds, the manger, and the city of Bethlehem. Some displays are very elaborate, with spotlights, running water, and recorded music. To say the least, they are intriguing works of art. During the Christmas holidays the Bethlehem people still continue the old custom of "going a-putzing," which is the gesture of calling on neighbors and friends to see their putz. All visitors are told the story of Christ's birth by the head of the house. Unfortunately, with the passing of each year there are fewer home putzes, but one can, and thousands do, visit the community putz in the Central Moravian Church.

When speaking of the Moravian Christmas, one thinks of the cookies that are served to those who come a-putzing. Moravians have their own traditional Brown Moravian Cookies* and White Christmas Cookies.* They are thin, crisp cookies cut with cutters that have been used in the same families for generations. With these, one also finds Filled Cookies,* Walnut Wafers,* Chocolate Jumbles,* Coconut Sugar Cookies* and Lebkuchen.*

Do all Pennsylvania Dutch housewives bake their own Christmas cookies? To be sure. Like the rest of Pennsylvania Dutch cookery, cookies have gained renown for their abundance. Many of the cookies are too pretty to eat, and some were not even meant for eating. Many Christmas trees are luscious with the cookies that hang on their branches. Cooks today bake up to sixty dozen Christmas cookies, but none attain the records of past generations when washbaskets as well as lard cans were filled with cookies. How long did they last? It was intended that they last at least through February, and once in a while they lasted until Easter! So many cookies, made from "pinches of this and handfuls of that."

No matter what the season, whenever you are in the Pennsylvania Dutch locale, listen for the words *Koom essa,* for that is the call to a Pennsylvania Dutch meal. You can expect plenty of food that is wonderful good!

Breadstuffs

THE first homemakers in the Pennsylvania Dutch country were so thrilled with the beautiful white flour that could be milled from the American wheat, in contrast to the dark flour they had been used to in Europe, that they were soon on a merry-go-round of constant baking. Poplar dough trays were made for the mixing and rising of bread dough, straw baskets woven for the final rising of the shaped loaf, and outdoor bake ovens built like the ones they had used in the Palatinate. Very few outdoor ovens are in existence today, and not many bread-baskets can be found, but the dough trays have not disappeared. In fact, they have attained a singular place of recognition. These rectangular wooden boxes have been turned into tables, now proudly displayed in living rooms. Wouldn't Grandma be surprised?

Every bride used a starter yeast that was given to her by her mother or neighbor. From this she made her own, always reserving a bit of dough or keeping the scrapings of the dough tray to use as a starter for the next baking. How much simpler breadmaking is today, yet only a few are left who continue to bake all their own bread.

The yeast dough that we Pennsylvania Dutch cooks turn into fancy rolls and sheet cakes fit perfectly into the category known today as coffeecakes. Our grandmothers never heard of *Kaffeklatches* but they certainly knew the art of baking the most delicious breads, rolls, and raised cakes.

HINTS ON BAKING YEAST BREADS

When using yeast recipes, have all ingredients at room temperature, since hot and cold ingredients kill yeast action. Yeast is always dissolved in lukewarm liquids.

To knead dough:

Press down and push dough with the heel of one hand. Then, with the other hand, lift the far side of the dough and fold. Rotate the dough with a quarter turn. Repeat the push, fold, and turn motions until the dough is smooth and elastic. It may be necessary to lightly flour the surface from time to time. Experience is the best aid in mastering the kneading technique.

In yeast baking, Pennsylvania Dutch cooks use mostly lard for their shortening. It makes breads richer and more flavorful. If vegetable shortening is substituted, the amount of shortening should be slightly increased.

WHITE BREAD

(2 loaves)

When kneading bread, Pennsylvania Dutch cooks mentally put into the dough the names of three friends. Is there a better time to bless one's friends?

1 package dry yeast
½ cup warm water
2 tablespoons shortening
2 cups scalded milk

2 tablespoons sugar
1½ teaspoons salt
about 7 cups sifted flour

Dissolve yeast in warm water. Add shortening to hot, scalded milk. While it is cooling, sift sugar and salt with the flour. When milk is lukewarm and shortening is melted, combine with yeast. Pour into large bowl containing about half of the flour mixture. Beat until smooth. Add remaining flour, mixing well. Turn onto floured board, adding more flour if dough is too sticky to knead. Knead for 10 minutes. (See Hints on Making Yeast Breads.)

Divide into 2 greased bread pans. Cover and let rise about 2 hours until doubled. Bake 50 minutes at 350°.

WHOLE WHEAT BREAD

(1 loaf)

2 packages dry yeast
1¼ cups warm water
2 tablespoons honey
2 tablespoons melted
butter
2 teaspoons salt

1½ cups unsifted whole
wheat flour
1½ cups sifted
all-purpose flour
1 tablespoon butter

Using a large mixing bowl, dissolve yeast in the warm water. Stir in honey and melted butter. Combine salt with the two kinds of flour. Add half of the flour to the yeast mixture and beat by hand 100 strokes or 3 minutes with electric mixer on medium setting. Add remaining flour and knead 2 minutes. Cover the bowl with a cloth and set in a warm place (85°) to rise until doubled in bulk, about 40 minutes. Press down dough and knead for 5 minutes. Place dough in a greased 9×5×3-inch loaf pan. Let rise another 40 minutes or until batter reaches top of pan. Bake 45 to 50 minutes in a preheated oven at 375°.

Remove from pan at once onto cooling rack. Brush top with butter.

RYE BREAD

(2 loaves)

Does anyone have hops? The original recipe, when given to me, called for "hop tea or its substitute—peach leaves tea." Since most of us do not have hops or peach trees growing in our yards, nor can we conveniently get hops from the brewery, let us be satisfied with buttermilk!

2 tablespoons lard	1 tablespoon salt
¾ cup buttermilk	¼ cup water
2 medium potatoes	2 cups rye flour
1 package dry yeast	5 cups sifted white flour
1 tablespoon sugar	1 tablespoon corn meal

Remove lard and buttermilk from refrigerator to warm to room temperature. Boil potatoes in salted water until soft. Drain and reserve 1 cup potato water. Mash potatoes. When potato water has cooled to *lukewarm*, sprinkle yeast into it and let it stand a few minutes. To dissolved yeast, add the sugar, salt, and lard. Gradually beat this liquid into the mashed potatoes. Add the buttermilk and water. Mix well. Beat in rye flour. Add white flour and mix well. Cover and let rise in warm place several hours until doubled in bulk.

Turn out on floured board and knead for 10 minutes. Place dough in 2 bread pans that have been greased and lightly sprinkled with corn meal. Cover and let rise again until doubled in size. Bake 30 minutes in 350° oven. Remove loaves from pans and wrap immediately in dampened cloths.

ROLLS

(2 dozen pan rolls)

¾ cup milk
¼ cup sugar
4 tablespoons lard
1 teaspoon salt
1 package dry yeast

¼ cup lukewarm water
1 egg, beaten
3½ cups flour
3 tablespoons butter

Scald the milk and pour it over the sugar, shortening, and salt in a mixing bowl. Sprinkle yeast over lukewarm water. When scalded-milk mixture has cooled to lukewarm, stir in the beaten egg, then the yeast. Stir until thoroughly blended. Add half of the flour. Beat until smooth. Add rest of the flour and mix well. Place in a greased bowl. Turn dough upside down so that top will be greased. Cover and let stand in a warm place until doubled in bulk, about 2 hours.

Press down and divide dough into 2 equal parts. Shape into 1½-inch balls and place in 2 greased 8-inch cake pans. Cover with a tea towel and let rise again, about 40 minutes.

Bake 20 minutes at 375°. Brush tops with butter. Reheat in a paper bag for 10 minutes in a 350° oven.

FASNACHTS

(5 dozen doughnuts)

Fasnachts are the Shrove Tuesday specialty. The dough is mixed and set to rise in the evening, then fried for breakfast on the morning of Shrove Tuesday. After you taste these you will say what the children say: "Why can't we have Shrove Tuesday more often?"

3 medium potatoes, peeled and quartered	1 cup potato water
1 cup milk	2 eggs, beaten
⅓ cup lard	about 9 cups sifted flour
¾ cup sugar	lard or other shortening
1 teaspoon salt	for deep-fat frying
1 package dry yeast	
2 tablespoons warm water (not hot)	

Cook peeled and quartered potatoes in salted water. Meanwhile, put the milk and lard in a small saucepan and heat to the boiling point. Remove from heat. Add sugar and salt, stirring until dissolved.

Sprinkle the yeast over the warm water and set aside.

When the potatoes are soft, drain and reserve 1 cup potato water. Mash the potatoes. To them add the 2 beaten eggs and the sweetened milk when it has cooled to lukewarm. Add the potato water and yeast. Stir in the flour, adding a few cups at a time until the dough is no longer sticky. Turn onto floured surface and knead well by repeatedly punching, stretching, and folding the dough over itself. When dough is smooth, put it in a large greased kettle or roaster. Cover and let rise overnight in a warm place, at least 70° and free from draft.

In the morning, on a floured surface, roll a quarter of the dough at a time to ⅓-inch thickness. Cut with a doughnut cutter or in 2×3-inch rectangles. If rectangles, cut a small slit in the center of each. Place on a tablecloth and cover with another cloth. As soon as the first ones are doubled in size, fry them in deep fat (375°). Drain on paper towels. Roll in granulated sugar.

Note: These are best when eaten the same day they are baked, so plan to share them.

FASNACHTS II

(36 3-inch doughnuts)

Delicious fasnachts with less than the usual 8-hour rising time. Start to finish time: 5 hours.

1 medium potato, pared and sliced	*2 eggs, well beaten*
½ teaspoon salt	*1 teaspoon salt*
2½ cups water	*1 package dry yeast*
¼ cup butter	*¼ cup warm water*
½ cup sugar	*6 cups sifted flour*
	granulated sugar

Cook pared and sliced potato in salted water until tender. Drain, saving 1½ cups potato water. Melt butter in this hot water. Mash the potato and measure ¼ cup. Using electric mixer, if you like, beat the potato with the sugar in a large mixing bowl until well blended. Add eggs and salt; mix well. Gradually add potato water. Dissolve yeast in ¼ cup warm water and add. Beat in half of the flour and then mix in the last 3 cups by hand. Dough will be soft.

Knead on well-floured surface until smooth and elastic. Place dough in greased bowl, then turn dough upside down so top surface is greased. Cover and let rise in a warm place, free from draft, until doubled in bulk, 2 to 3 hours.

Turn onto floured surface and knead 1 minute. Divide dough in half. Roll each half into a rectangle ⅓ inch thick. With pastry wheel or knife cut into 2×3-inch rectangles, making slits an inch long in the center of each. Place on a tablecloth, away from any draft, and cover with a cloth to rise again until doubled in size, about 1 hour.

Fry a few at a time in deep fat at 375°. Drain on paper towels. Roll in granulated sugar.

CRULLERS

(4 dozen)

Another potato doughnut, but without yeast. An excellent item for dunking!

3 eggs	5 teaspoons baking
1½ cups sugar	powder
2 tablespoons melted	½ teaspoon salt
butter	1 cup milk
1 cup mashed potatoes	2 teaspoons vanilla
5 cups flour	confectioners' sugar

Beat eggs in a large mixing bowl. Add sugar, butter, and potatoes, beating well after each addition. Sift together the flour, baking powder, and salt. Add these to the butter mixture alternately with the milk. Stir in the vanilla. Roll out on floured surface to ½-inch thickness. Cut with doughnut cutter and fry in deep fat (375°). Drain on unglazed paper or paper towels. Using shaker or sieve, shake confectioners' sugar over the crullers.

FOLK FESTIVAL FASNACHTS

(3 dozen)

4 eggs	1½ teaspoons salt
2 cups sugar	½ teaspoon soda
½ cup shortening,	2 cups buttermilk
melted	shortening for deep-fat
8 cups sifted flour	frying
3 tablespoons baking	powdered sugar
powder	

Beat the eggs in a large bowl. Add the sugar and beat well. Stir in the melted shortening until well blended. Sift together the remaining dry ingredients. Add the dry ingredients alternately with the buttermilk. If dough seems too sticky, knead in a bit more flour on floured surface before you roll it. Roll half at a time to ½-inch thickness. Cut in 2×3-inch rectangles. Cut a slit in the center of each. Fry in deep fat (375°). Drain on unglazed paper.

To serve: Dust them with powdered sugar.

SOUR CREAM DOUGHNUTS

(1½ dozen)

1½ cups sour cream
1 egg, beaten
about 4 cups flour
¼ cup sugar

1 teaspoon baking
powder
confectioners' sugar or
all purpose syrup

Mix together the sour cream and beaten egg. Stir in the flour, sugar, and baking powder that have been sifted together.

If necessary to roll easily, add more flour. Turn out on floured board and roll ½ inch thick. Cut in 2×3-inch rectangles with a cut slit in the center. Fry in deep fat (360°) until brown on both sides. Drain on unglazed paper.

To serve: Sprinkle with confectioners' sugar or split doughnuts and spread with syrup.

RAISED CAKES

(4 8-inch cakes)

A cake worthy of your freezer! Pennsylvania Dutch cooks mix these excellent coffeecakes the day before baking. If you don't do this, give yourself an early-morning start.

2 medium-sized
potatoes, peeled and
quartered
1 cup sugar
1 package dry yeast
¼ cup lukewarm water
½ cup lard
¼ cup butter

½ cup potato water
½ cup sugar
2 eggs, beaten
½ teaspoon salt
7 cups flour
Crumb Topping* or
Silver Dollar Topping*

Cook peeled and quartered potatoes in salted water for 25 minutes. Drain liquid from potatoes, but save ½ cup to use later. Mash potatoes and add 1 cup sugar, stirring until sugar is melted. Dissolve yeast in ¼ cup lukewarm water. Add to potatoes when they have cooled to lukewarm temperature. Stir until blended. Cover and set aside in a warm place, about 80°, free from any draft.

After 2 hours, proceed again as follows: In a saucepan, heat the lard, butter, potato water, and sugar until the lard is melted and sugar dissolved. Cool to lukewarm. Add this lukewarm shortening to potato-yeast mixture. Add beaten eggs, salt, and 3 cups of flour and beat until smooth. Mix in remaining flour and knead until smooth and elastic. Put into large greased bowl or roast pan. Cover and set in a warm place (80°), free from draft, for at least 6 hours or overnight.

Turn out on floured board and divide into 4 parts. Flatten into rounds 1 inch high. Place in 4 round 8-inch pans. Cover with a cloth and let rise 1 to 2 hours or until doubled in size. While these are rising, prepare following crumb topping.

CRUMB TOPPING FOR RAISED CAKES:

1 cup sugar
½ cup flour

¼ cup butter
1 teaspoon cinnamon

Mix together into fine crumbs. Brush risen cakes with sweetened water: 1 teaspoon sugar to 3 tablespoons water. Top with crumbs. Bake 20 minutes in a 350° oven. Serve with butter.

SILVER DOLLAR TOPPING FOR RAISED CAKES:

(*A substitute for Crumb Topping*)
(Enough for 4 cakes)

To be refrigerated at least 8 hours before slicing.

1 cup sugar
½ cup flour
½ cup melted butter

Mix ingredients and form into a roll 1 inch in diameter. Wrap in wax paper or foil and refrigerate 8 or more hours. Slice into thin slices and place on top of raised cakes which have been brushed with sweetened water. Bake cakes 20 minutes at 350°.

BISCUITS

(12 medium-size)

2 cups flour
4 teaspoons baking
powder
1 teaspoon salt

3 tablespoons
shortening
¾ cup milk

Sift together the dry ingredients. Blend in shortening with your fingers. Add the milk slowly and mix. Beat for 30 seconds. Drop into greased muffin pans, ¾ full. Or, roll out on a slightly floured board to ½-inch thickness and cut with a biscuit cutter. Bake 12 to 15 minutes in a 425° oven.

CORN MUFFINS

(9 muffins)

In this regional cookery only roasted yellow corn meal is used. It is the preference for muffins, mush, scrapple, hot cakes, and corn pone.

¾ *cup corn meal*
¾ *cup flour*
½ *cup sugar*
1½ *teaspoons baking powder*

¼ *teaspoon salt*
¾ *cup milk*
¼ *cup butter, melted*
1 *egg*

Mix all ingredients together and beat for 2 minutes. Bake in greased muffin pans for 25 to 30 minutes in a 350° oven.

RICE MUFFINS

(18 2-inch muffins)

¾ *cup cooked rice*
1 *cup milk*
1 *egg, well beaten*
2 *tablespoons butter, melted*

2¼ *cups flour*
5 *teaspoons baking powder*
3 *tablespoons sugar*
½ *teaspoon salt*

Combine first 4 ingredients. Sift together dry ingredients. Add liquid to the dry ingredients, stirring just enough to dampen flour. Drop by spoonfuls into greased muffin pans. Bake 20 minutes in 400° oven.

STICKY BUNS

(4 8-inch rounds, 10 rolls each)

2 cups scalded milk
½ cup lard
1½ teaspoons salt
½ cup sugar
1 package dry yeast
¼ cup warm water
about 9 cups flour

4 tablespoons butter,
  melted
¾ cup sugar
1 teaspoon cinnamon
12 tablespoons butter
1⅓ cups brown sugar

To the scalded milk add the lard, salt, and sugar and stir until the lard is melted. Dissolve the yeast in the warm water. When the milk has cooled to lukewarm, add the yeast to it. Add the flour, enough to make a soft dough. Knead thoroughly until it no longer sticks to the board. Put into a greased bowl. Turn dough upside down so that top is greased. Cover with a cloth and let rise in a warm place (80°) several hours until it triples in bulk.

Roll into a rectangle 12×24 inches. Spread with melted butter, ¾ cup sugar, and 1 teaspoon cinnamon. Roll up like a jelly roll. Cut roll into 4 parts and each part into 10 slices. Into each of 4 greased 8-inch pans dot 3 tablespoons butter over the bottom and cover with ⅓ cup brown sugar. Place 10 rolls, cut side up, into each pan. Cover pans again and let rise until almost doubled in size.

Bake 20 to 25 minutes in a 375° oven. Invert on plates as soon as you remove from oven.

SCHWENKFELDER CAKE

(2 10×13-inch sheet cakes)

A saffron-flavored yeast cake that is the traditional wedding cake of the Schwenkfelders, a religious sect who came to Pennsylvania in 1734 and settled in the Perkiomen Valley.

These cakes are usually mixed in the evening and set to rise overnight.

STEP I:

> 2 potatoes, peeled and   1 package yeast
>   quartered   ½ cup potato water
> ½ cup sugar

Cook peeled and quartered potatoes in salted water until soft. Drain potatoes, reserving ½ cup potato water. Combine sugar and potatoes. Dissolve yeast in *lukewarm* potato water. Stir into potatoes. Cover and let set in warm place to rise.

STEP II:

> ¼ cup hot water   1 egg
> ½ teaspoon saffron   1 cup sugar
> ½ cup lard   ½ teaspoon salt
> 1 cup warm milk   2 cups flour

After the sponge has set for 3 hours, pour hot water on the saffron and let stand a few minutes. Meanwhile, soften the lard in warm milk. Add it to egg beaten with sugar and salt. Stir in the saffron water. Add this and 2 cups flour to the light potato sponge and beat until smooth. Cover and let rise in a 75° temperature, free from drafts.

STEP III:

6 cups flour
1 cup light brown
   sugar
⅓ cup lard

1 teaspoon cinnamon
1 cup flour
¼ cup cream

After the sponge has risen for 8 hours, add the 6 cups of flour (even more, if necessary, to handle). Knead on floured board until smooth. Divide dough and roll into 2 cakes, about 10×13 inches. Place on cookie sheets and cover with a cloth to rise ½ hour. Rub together the brown sugar, lard, cinnamon and flour to make crumbs. When cakes are risen, brush with cream and top with crumbs. Bake in 350° oven for 20 to 25 minutes.

POTATO BUNS

(3 dozen)

A delicious crumb topping makes these extra-special.

3 medium potatoes
1 package dry yeast
¼ cup warm water
½ cup lard
½ cup sugar
2 eggs, beaten

1 teaspoon salt
5 cups flour, unsifted
¼ cup sugar
¼ cup flour
1 tablespoon butter

Have all ingredients at room temperature. Peel and quarter potatoes, then cook in salted water. When potatoes are soft, sprinkle yeast into ¼ cup warm (not hot) water. Drain potatoes but reserve ¼ cup potato water. Mash potatoes. Add lard and sugar to the potatoes, beating until lard is melted and the potato mixture is smooth. Add the beaten eggs, potato water, and salt, and mix well. Stir in the dissolved yeast, then half of the flour. Turn onto floured working surface and knead in 2½ remaining cups of flour. Place in large greased bowl or kettle. Cover. Let rise in a draft-free spot, 75 to 80°, for about 2 hours or until doubled in bulk.

Turn dough onto floured surface again and knead 2 minutes. Shape into balls 2 inches in diameter. Place in 3 greased 8-inch cake pans, with buns barely touching. Cover with towels and let rise again. Make crumbs with ¼ cup sugar, ¼ cup flour, and 1 tablespoon butter. When cakes have risen 40 minutes, brush top with sweetened water (1 teaspoon sugar in 3 tablespoons water). Top with crumbs. In 350° oven, bake 20 minutes.

MORAVIAN SUGAR CAKE

(3 11×15-inch sheet cakes)

2 or 3 potatoes	2 eggs, slightly beaten
1 package dry yeast	7 cups sifted flour
⅔ cup warm water	2 cups light brown
1 cup milk, scalded	sugar
½ cup sugar	½ pound butter
1½ teaspoons salt	cinnamon
½ cup butter	

Peel and cook enough potatoes to make 1 cup mashed potatoes. Dissolve yeast in ⅔ cup warm water. Scald milk, then add sugar, salt, and butter, stirring until dissolved. Cool until lukewarm. Add the mashed potatoes, yeast, and eggs, beating until smooth. Add the flour and knead 10 minutes, using more flour as dough becomes sticky. Place in a greased bowl. Turn dough upside down so greased part is on top. Cover and let rise in a warm place (80°) about 1¼ hours or until doubled in bulk. Turn out on floured board and divide into 3 parts. Roll each part into a 11×15-inch cake and then place on cookie sheets. Cover and let rise to ¾-inch thickness.

Using the 2 cups of light brown sugar, sprinkle it over the 3 cakes. Punch dough with thumbs to make holes one inch apart. Place ¼-inch cube of butter in each hole, reserving 2 tablespoons of the ½ pound of butter to melt and sprinkle over the top with a pastry brush. Sprinkle with cinnamon. Bake at 350° for 20 to 25 minutes. Cool before serving.

BUTTER SEMMEL BUNS

(3 dozen)

Butter Semmel Buns betray the secrets of our cooks. They use much butter in their cooking.

1 package dry yeast
½ cup lukewarm water
1 cup scalded milk
1 cup butter
½ cup sugar
¼ teaspoon cinnamon

1 teaspoon salt
1 egg, beaten
about 6 cups sifted flour
¼ pound butter
¾ cup cinnamon sugar

Dissolve yeast in warm water. Keep at a temperature of 70°. Meanwhile, scald milk. To hot milk add butter, sugar, cinnamon, salt, and beaten egg. As soon as sponge begins to look like waves, mix with milk mixture. Stir in flour and mix well. Let rise in a greased bowl until double in bulk (about 2 hours).

Turn out on floured board and knead until smooth, adding more flour if necessary. Roll out to ⅜-inch thickness and cut into 2- or 3-inch squares. In center of each square place bits of butter and a teaspoon of cinnamon sugar. Fold opposite corners to center and press together. Place on tins to rise another hour.

Bake 15 minutes in 375° oven. Brush with melted butter and sprinkle with sugar. Serve warm.

SCHTEEPERS

(3 8-inch coffeecakes)

1 cake yeast	*3 tablespoons cream*
2 cups warm water	*2 tablespoons flour*
½ cup lard	*2 tablespoons sugar*
1 cup sugar	*1 tablespoon butter*
1 teaspoon salt	*cinnamon*
7 cups sifted flour	

Combine the first 6 ingredients in the order given and beat until smooth. Put dough into a greased bowl. Cover. Let rise in a warm place, free from draft, for several hours until double in bulk. Press down and work into 3 8-inch cake pans, well greased. Cover with a cloth and let rise again.

When double in bulk, brush top with cream and sprinkle with crumbs made from rubbing together the remaining flour, sugar, and butter. Sprinkle with cinnamon. Bake 35 minutes at 375°.

CINNAMON FLOP

(1 8-inch square cake)

1½ cups sugar	*2 teaspoons baking*
2 tablespoons melted	*powder*
butter	*1 cup milk*
1 egg, beaten	*1 cup brown sugar*
2 cups flour	*4 tablespoons butter*
	cinnamon

Cream together the 1½ cups sugar with the 2 tablespoons melted butter. Add beaten egg. Sift flour and baking powder together and add alternately with milk to sugar and butter mixture. Spread evenly in greased 8×8-inch pan. Cover with brown sugar and dot with 4 tablespoons butter. Sprinkle generously with cinnamon. Bake 30 minutes at 425°. Cut into squares and serve warm.

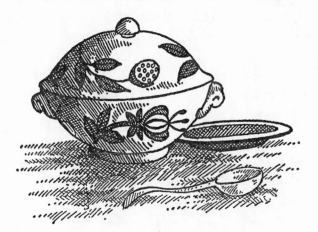

Soups

ALL Pennsylvania Dutch soups are served as the main course of supper and never as the pre-entree course for dinner. Many of the soups we have could very well be called stews. We like thick soups that have plenty of "stuff" in them. No broth or bouillon, thank you. Into the soups we put *rivvels* (literally, lumps), noodles,* knepp,* and Dough balls.* When served, crackers, pretzels, or even popcorn are added. Brown Flour Potato Soup,* and Milk Rivvel Soup* are the simplest. We call them the poor man's soups. For guests we are more likely to serve Chicken Corn Soup,* Old-Fashioned Bean Soup (with ham),* or Calf's Head Soup.* They are most delicious even when we are utilizing the chicken carcass or the ham bone.

KNEPP FOR SOUP

(*Little dumplings*)

(6 servings)

1 tablespoon butter	¼ teaspoon salt
3 tablespoons flour	2 tablespoons water

Crumble together the butter, flour, and salt. Moisten with the water. Stir and beat until the mass forms a smooth ball. Drop tiny bits of knepp, just about ⅛ teaspoonful at a time, into the boiling broth or soup. Boil for 5 minutes.

CHICKEN CORN SOUP

(Serves 8)

This is tops in good eating. In Lancaster County the Ladies of the Fire Company Auxiliaries have gained renown for their Chicken Corn Soup suppers. Long lines form outside the firehouse awaiting word that the soup is being served.

1 4-pound stewing chicken, cut up	2 cups fresh or frozen corn
2 teaspoons salt	1 tablespoon chopped parsley
⅛ teaspoon pepper	
½ teaspoon saffron	2 hard-cooked eggs, chopped
2 cups noodles	

In a large stewing kettle, cover the cut-up chicken with 3 quarts water. Add the salt, pepper, and saffron. Stew until tender. Remove chicken from stock and set aside the breast and legs for future potpie. (You can reserve 1 cup of stock also, if you wish.) Bone the rest of the chicken, cut into small pieces, and return to stock to chill thoroughly. Before reheating, skim off most of the fat from the top. Add noodles and corn. Boil 15 minutes longer. Add the parsley and chopped eggs before serving.

Note: Knepp* may be substituted for noodles, if desired. Recipe above.

CHICKEN NOODLE SOUP
(Serves 8)

Chicken Soup is no better than its chicken. For good soup a fat stewing chicken is a must. Do not try to make good soup with a fryer. The ideal procedure is to stew and bone the chicken one day, then skim the fat off the chilled broth the following day.

*4-pound stewing
  chicken
3 quarts water
2 teaspoons salt
2 whole stems of celery*

*½ teaspoon saffron
⅛ teaspoon pepper
8 ounces noodles*
1 tablespoon minced
  parsley*

Cut up the chicken, if whole, and stew with the seasonings in the 3 quarts water. When tender, remove chicken and bone. Add meat and noodles to broth and simmer slowly for 30 minutes. Add parsley just before serving.

BEEF NOODLE SOUP
(Serves 8)

Prepare as Chicken Noodle Soup but substitute 1 soup bone and 2 pounds boiling beef for the chicken, and omit the saffron.

PHILADELPHIA PEPPERPOT

(Serves 6)

This recipe has been used in one family for over a hundred years. They made it by the gallon "because it tastes even better when reheated."

1 veal shin
2 quarts water
1 pound boiled tripe
½ cup chopped onion
2 teaspoons salt
⅛ teaspoon black pepper
1 teaspoon parsley flakes

just a dash of cayenne pepper
Dumplings for soup*
2 cups diced raw potato
2 tablespoons flour
½ cup water
1 teaspoon marjoram

Cook veal in 2 quarts water for about 2 hours. When meat is tender, partially cool it and bone. With a scissors, cut tripe into ¼-inch squares and cook with the onion and seasonings for 25 minutes. Make dumplings. (Recipe follows.) Return veal to broth. Add potatoes and cook 15 minutes. In a shaker, mix flour and water and add to soup while stirring. Add dumplings and marjoram. Boil just 5 minutes longer.

DUMPLINGS FOR SOUP

(6 servings)

1 cup flour
½ teaspoon salt
1 teaspoon baking powder

1 tablespoon melted butter
1 egg, beaten
¼ cup milk

Sift together the flour, salt, and baking powder. Stir in the melted butter, then the combined egg and milk. Drop batter from a teaspoon into boiling soup. Cover and boil for 15 minutes.

MILK RIVVEL SOUP

(Serves 4)

Often called "the poor man's soup."

1 quart milk	*1 cup flour*
2 tablespoons butter	*½ teaspoon salt*
½ teaspoon salt	*1 egg, well beaten*
pepper to taste	

Heat milk in a 2-quart saucepan with butter, salt, and pepper. Combine flour, salt, and egg. Rub through the hands into the hot milk. Turn heat to low and simmer for 5 minutes.

MOCK CHICKEN SOUP

(Serves 8)

1 veal shin (with meat)	*1 onion*
4 quarts water	*2 stems celery*
1 tablespoon salt	*1 cup rice*
¼ teaspoon pepper	*1 teaspoon parsley flakes*

Simmer the veal shin in 4 quarts water for 3 hours. Lift out meat and bone. Strain broth. Remove meat from bone and cut into bite-size pieces. Return strained broth to kettle. Add seasonings, onion, and celery. Bring to a boil. Add rice and parsley. Boil slowly for ½ hour. Add more salt, if desired.

CHICKEN RIVVEL SOUP

(Serves 6)

The word *rivvel* means "lump"—and this soup is full of lumps that look like rice.

1 cup flour	*4 cups chicken broth*
½ teaspoon salt	*2 cups corn (optional)*
1 egg, well beaten	

Combine the flour, salt, and beaten egg. Rub through the hands into boiling chicken broth. Add corn and simmer for 15 minutes.

BEAN SOUP WITH BEEF

(Serves 6)

1 pound dried pea	*¼ cup chopped onion*
beans	*¼ teaspoon cloves*
1 soup bone with meat	*(optional)*
on it	*¼ teaspoon allspice*
2 teaspoons salt	*(optional)*
¼ teaspoon pepper	*Dough Balls* (optional)*
3 medium-size potatoes,	
diced	

Soak the dried beans in water overnight. Cook the soup bone in water with salt and pepper added for several hours until the meat is tender. Remove the bone, cut off the meat, and cook the beans in the broth until they are soft. Add the meat, diced potatoes, onion, spices, and dough balls. Simmer 25 minutes.

OLD-FASHIONED BEAN SOUP

(Serves 8)

This one utilizes the leftover ham bone and ham.

1 pound dried pea beans	*¼ teaspoon pepper*
1 ham bone	*4 potatoes, diced*
1 cup leftover ham	*¼ cup chopped onion*
2 teaspoons salt	*1 tablespoon parsley*

Soak the beans in water overnight. In the morning, drain. Cook the ham bone and beans for several hours in 2 quarts water. When the beans are nearly soft, add the rest of the ingredients. Simmer until the potatoes are soft.

CALF'S HEAD SOUP

(Serves 8)

Our grandmothers used a calf's head for this delicious soup, but today a veal shin is used more often. Made with either, it is extra-special: a spicy soup, full of meat, potatoes, and dough balls, all dutifully seasoned with the flavor of brown flour.

1 veal shin or 1 calf's head	*½ cup flour*
	½ teaspoon marjoram
3 potatoes, peeled and diced	*¼ teaspoon cloves*
	¼ teaspoon allspice
1 medium-size onion, diced	*2 hard-cooked eggs, chopped*
½ pound fresh sausage meat	*2 tablespoons butter*
	Dough Balls*

Cook the veal shin or calf's head in 2 quarts water for several hours. After 2 hours of cooking, or when meat is almost tender, prepare other ingredients.

Cook potatoes and onion for 20 minutes in 1 quart water with ½ teaspoon salt. Meanwhile, shape sausage into ½-inch balls and fry until brown.

Make dough balls as in the following recipe. When the meat is tender, remove from the broth, cool slightly, then take off the bone and cut into small pieces. In a heavy skillet brown the flour over medium heat, stirring constantly. Stir in 1 cup broth to make a smooth paste. Add it to the broth with the meat, potatoes, sausage balls, spices, chopped eggs, butter, and dough balls. Simmer 5 minutes.

DOUGH BALLS

(25 ½-inch balls)

Excellent bites of goodness to be put into Calf's Head Soup* or Bean Soup.*

 1 cup flour   3 tablespoons water
 ½ teaspoon salt   2 tablespoons butter
 3 tablespoons lard

Sift together the flour and salt. Cut the lard into the flour until it is the size of peas. Toss lightly in the bowl while adding the water gradually. With floured hands, shape into tiny balls, ½ inch in diameter. Brown in 2 tablespoons of melted butter over low heat, turning frequently. When nicely browned, add to soup.

BROWN FLOUR POTATO SOUP

(Serves 6)

Brown flour soups have a flavor all their own and are well worth your trying if you have never tasted them. Flour is browned with butter in a heavy skillet until almost burnt. The browner the flour, the better the flavor.

4 large potatoes	*2 tablespoons butter*
1 onion, chopped fine	*salt and pepper to taste*
1 quart milk	*1 hard-cooked egg,*
4 tablespoons flour	*chopped*

Dice the potatoes and cook with the onion in salted water until tender. Add the milk. Brown the flour in melted butter in a heavy frying pan, stirring constantly until well browned. Bring the potatoes and milk to a boil, then stir in the browned flour and boil a few minutes until it thickens. Season to taste. Lastly, add chopped hard-cooked egg.

POTATO SOUP

(Serves 6)

Potato Soup of one kind or another is one of the most popular among the Pennsylvania Dutch.

1 small onion	*1 tablespoon flour*
1 stem celery	*2 tablespoons butter*
3 medium potatoes	*2 tablespoons parsley,*
1 quart water	*cut fine*
1½ teaspoons salt	*1 hard-cooked egg,*
black pepper to taste	*chopped*
2 cups milk	

Chop onion and celery. Peel and dice potatoes in ½-inch cubes. Put onion, celery, and potatoes in 2-quart saucepan with 1 quart water, 1½ teaspoons salt, and pepper to taste. Cook 20 minutes; then add 1 cup milk.

In a shaker, mix flour with other cup of milk. Add to soup, stirring until it comes to a boil. Let boil 1 minute. Add butter, parsley, and chopped hard-cooked egg.

CORN SOUP

(Serves 4)

"Just picked this morning" is the call of the corn huckster as he goes through town. For this soup and other fresh corn dishes, the Pennsylvania Dutch insist on using corn the same day it is picked.

6 ears fresh corn	*2 cups milk*
1 cup water	*2 tablespoons butter*
1 teaspoon sugar	*4 slices bread*
1 teaspoon salt	

Cut corn off the cob and cook 10 minutes in 1 cup water with sugar and salt. Add milk and butter. When thoroughly heated, serve thus: one piece of bread is placed in each soup bowl and the soup is poured over it. The bread absorbs the thin liquid and makes a delicious supper dish.

SALSIFY SOUP

(Serves 4)

A vegetable oyster soup that has the full flavor of oyster stew, without even one oyster!

5 *medium salsify roots*	1 *tablespoon butter*
1 *cup water*	⅛ *teaspoon pepper*
3 *cups milk*	1 *teaspoon salt*

Scrape roots and slice in ¼-inch slices. Cook slowly in 1 cup water until tender, about 20 minutes. Add milk, butter, and seasoning. Bring to a boil. Serve with crackers.

CREAM OF TOMATO SOUP

(Serves 6)

2 *tablespoons butter*	1 *quart milk*
2 *tablespoons flour*	2 *cups canned tomato*
1 *teaspoon salt*	*juice*
⅛ *teaspoon pepper*	¼ *teaspoon baking soda*
1 *tablespoon grated onion*	

Melt the butter, then remove from heat and add flour, seasonings, and onion. Blend thoroughly. Slowly stir in 1 cup of the milk.

In another saucepan, heat the tomato juice. When it begins to boil, remove from heat, add soda, and stir. Now add the rest of the milk to the white sauce and bring to a boil, stirring constantly. To avoid curdling, let the sauce stand 5 minutes. Then add the tomato juice very, very slowly to the white sauce, stirring constantly.

PEA SOUP

(Serves 4)

1 pound fresh peas	*2 tablespoons flour*
2 cups water	*2 cups milk*
½ teaspoon sugar	*½ teaspoon salt*
½ teaspoon salt	*½ teaspoon sugar*
4 tablespoons butter	*dash of pepper*

Shell peas and cook 20 minutes in 2 cups water with ½ teaspoon each of sugar and salt. While peas are cooking, make the cream sauce by melting the butter, blending in the flour, and adding milk and seasonings. Cook the sauce over medium heat until it boils and thickens, stirring constantly. When peas are tender, add to sauce and serve.

VEGETABLE SOUP I

(Serves 4)

Only four vegetables in this one, yet most delicious.

1½ pounds chuck or	*2 small onions, diced*
other beef with bone	*3 stems of celery, cut*
1 teaspoon salt	*2 large carrots, sliced*
¼ teaspoon pepper	*1 tablespoon brown*
6 cups cold water	*sugar*
2 cups canned tomatoes	

Cut beef into 1-inch cubes and put in large kettle with the bone. Add salt, pepper, and water. Bring to a boil and simmer for 2 hours. Add remaining ingredients and simmer for another 45 minutes.

VEGETABLE SOUP II
(Serves 8)

2 quarts water	2 cups tomatoes
1 tablespoon salt	1 cup chopped cabbage
¼ teaspoon pepper	1 cup peas
2 pounds beef shank	1 cup beans
bone with some meat	1 cup carrots
3 potatoes	⅓ cup rice
1 onion	2 tablespoons minced
½ cup cut celery	parsley

Add the water, salt, and pepper to soup bone and beef. Bring to a boil and simmer 2 to 3 hours. Add vegetables and rice and cook a half-hour longer. Just before serving, add parsley.

CREAM OF VEGETABLE SOUP
(Serves 6)

½ cup celery, diced	2 tablespoons butter
½ cup carrots, diced	2 cups water
½ cup green beans,	1½ teaspoons salt
diced	black pepper
½ cup peas	2 cups milk
1 cup diced potatoes	1 tablespoon flour
¼ cup chopped onion	

Cook all the vegetables together with the butter, water, salt, and pepper for 25 minutes. Add 1 cup milk. Mix other cup milk with the flour in a shaker. Stir in the flour and milk, stirring constantly until the soup boils again and thickens.

CLAM SOUP
(Serves 6)

1 small onion
4 medium potatoes
1 quart water
1½ teaspoons salt
pepper to taste
2 dozen clams

2 cups milk
2 tablespoons butter
8 saltines, crushed
2 hard-cooked eggs,
   chopped

Dice onion and potatoes and cook in the water, with salt and pepper added, for 20 minutes. Meanwhile, mince clams or put through food chopper. Cook clams with potatoes for 5 minutes. Add milk, butter, saltines, and chopped, hard-cooked eggs. Stir and serve.

CLAM CORN SOUP
(Serves 6)

2 medium potatoes
1 onion
3 cups water
1 teaspoon salt
dash pepper
2 dozen clams
2 cups whole-kernel corn

2 cups milk
2 tablespoons butter
1 hard-cooked egg,
   chopped fine
1 tablespoon chopped
   parsley

Dice the potatoes and onion. Cook in 3 cups water with seasonings. Put clams through food chopper. When potatoes are almost soft, add clams and corn to them and cook together for another 5 minutes. Add milk and butter and simmer a few minutes more. Add the egg, chopped fine, with parsley just before serving, or use as a garnish on top of the soup.

OYSTER STEW

(Serves 4)

1 pint oysters
3 tablespoons butter
1 quart milk
1 teaspoon salt

pepper
pretzels and oyster
   crackers

Heat the drained oysters in butter until the edges begin to curl. In another saucepan heat the milk and season with salt and pepper. Add oysters to hot milk. Serve with pretzels and oyster crackers.

COLD SUPPER SOUP

(Serves 6)

6 slices white bread
1 quart fresh raspberries,
   strawberries, or
   blackberries

6 tablespoons sugar
1½ quarts milk

Break the bread into small pieces and put into individual soup dishes or one large bowl. Put fruit and sugar on the bread. Pour milk over it and serve immediately.

Meat and Cheese

Three times a day! Yes, one eats meat and potatoes three times a day on the farms in eastern Pennsylvania. For breakfast there is usually fried Scrapple,* meat pudding, or ham. Fresh and smoked sausage find a place here, too, as well as creamed dried beef made with brown flour.

Dinners usually center around a roast, fresh ham, beef, or veal, or perhaps a platter of browned canned pork tenderloin. We like our boiled dinners, too. When potatoes are cooked in the same pot with the boiled beef and turnips, ham and beans, or ham and cabbage, we call that "good eating."

The meat for supper is usually cold meat, sliced down from

the boiled ham or the cooked roll of beef. There is no fear about lack of protein in this diet. The supper meal is also the time when Pennsylvania Dutch cheeses are enjoyed. These are cheeses that are unusual.

Schmierkase,* although very creamy, is akin to cottage cheese. Other cheeses we make are unique. Egg Cheese* is made in those fancy heart molds now found on the shelves of the antique shops. Egg cheese is also called sweet curd, but must not be confused with either Pennsylvania Dutch ball cheese or cup cheese. Further explanation of the cheeses will be found with the cheese recipes at the end of this chapter.

CHICKEN POTPIE

(Serves 6)

Chicken Potpie is delicious when a large stewing chicken is used. It must be a chicken that has been fattened. Young fryers will not make a flavorful potpie.

4 to 5-pound stewing chicken	4 medium potatoes, peeled and quartered
3 quarts water	2 medium sweet potatoes, peeled and cut
2 teaspoons salt	
¼ teaspoon pepper	
1 teaspoon saffron (optional)	4 small onions, quartered
½ cup cut celery	¼ cup chopped parsley Potpie*

Cook chicken in 3 quarts water with salt, pepper, saffron, and celery for several hours until it is tender. Remove chicken to bone it and replace with potatoes and onions. Cook for 15 minutes. Add parsley.

Make Potpie and drop squares, one by one, over chicken and

potatoes. If there is not enough broth to cover Potpie squares, add boiling water. Cover and cook for 20 minutes more. If desired, thicken broth with ¼ cup flour dissolved in ½ cup water.

BAKED CHICKEN POTPIE

(Serves 8)

When Mother announced potpie for dinner, we always wondered whether it would be boiled or baked. Some of us hoped for a baked potpie, while others begged for the boiled. Baked to a golden brown with rich juice bubbling through the crust, this potpie will tempt even the poorest of appetites.

*4-pound stewing
  chicken
Pastry for Two-Crust
  Pie**
*5 medium potatoes,
  peeled and quartered*

*1 minced onion
2 tablespoons minced
  parsley
salt and pepper to taste*

Cook the chicken in salted water until tender (several hours). When tender, remove from broth and bone. Line bottom and side of a 6×10-inch baking dish with pastry. Fill with layers of chicken, raw potatoes, onion, parsley, salt, and pepper. (You won't need all of the chicken.) Pour enough of the chicken broth over the top to almost cover. Cover with pastry top, fastening edges securely. Cut holes in the lid to allow steam to escape. Bake at 350° for 1 hour.

CHICKEN CORN PIE

(Serves 8)

Prepare as Baked Chicken Potpie* but substitute 2 cups fresh or frozen corn for the potatoes.

PRESSED CHICKEN

(Serves 8)

Here is a company supper dish. Mother served it on hot days when she didn't want to "bring up the coal fire" to cook meat.

Cut up a chicken in the usual manner and place in a kettle that has a tight-fitting lid to keep in the steam. Cover with 2 cups water and season with salt and pepper. Cover and let it cook slowly until meat will easily fall from the bones. Discard skin, bone, and gristle. Cut meat into small pieces. Put into a loaf pan, pouring the broth over it. The loaf will jell when chilled and can then be sliced. Serve cold.

CHICKEN LOAF

(Serves 4 to 6)

If you could see how clean the chickens are when brought to the Reading and Lancaster markets, you would want to eat chicken as often as the Pennsylvania Dutch people do. Chickens are scrubbed clean, with never a pinfeather to be seen.

2 cups cooked chicken	⅔ teaspoon salt
1 cup soft breadcrumbs	2 eggs, well beaten
2 tablespoons parsley	1 cup milk
2 tablespoons chopped celery	3 tablespoons melted butter

Mix all ingredients in the order given. Pour into a buttered loaf pan. Bake 30 minutes in a 375° oven.

BOILED BEEF POTPIE

(Serves 8)

We make Pork and Veal Potpies, too, using this recipe.

*1½ to 2 pounds
  stewing beef
2 onions, quartered
2 tablespoons finely
  chopped parsley*

*1½ teaspoons salt
1 teaspoon marjoram
4 medium potatoes
Potpie*
black pepper*

Cut meat into cubes and cook in boiling water until tender, about 1½ hours. Add onions, parsley, salt, and marjoram.

Pare potatoes and slice in ¼-inch slices. Prepare Potpie. Roll out half of potpie dough. Drop into broth a layer of potatoes, using half of them, and then the potpie squares for next layer. Let come to a boil; stir. Roll remainder of dough and add it and remaining potatoes. Sprinkle with pepper.

Add boiling water, if necessary, to keep broth boiling up through potpie. Cover and cook for 20 minutes without removing lid.

BOILED BEEF AND TURNIPS

(Serves 6)

Grandma used to say, "It takes a heavy frost to give turnips a good, sweet flavor."

*1 pound lean beef
  cubes
1 teaspoon salt
¼ teaspoon pepper*

*8 turnips
3 potatoes
2 tablespoons butter*

Simmer beef cubes slowly for an hour in just enough water to cover. Season and add peeled and quartered turnips and potatoes with butter, adding more water if necessary. Cook slowly for 30 minutes.

PENNSYLVANIA DUTCH MEAT LOAF

(Serves 8)

2 pounds ground beef	*2 cups soft breadcrumbs*
½ pound ground pork	*1 medium onion,*
½ pound ground veal	*chopped*
3 eggs	*2 teaspoons salt*
2 cups milk	*⅛ teaspoon pepper*

Have the butcher grind the 3 meats together. Beat the eggs and add the milk to them. Soak the breadcrumbs in this mixture for about 5 minutes. Mix together thoroughly the meat, crumbs, and seasonings.

Turn into a roast pan and shape into a loaf. Bake 1½ to 2 hours at 375°.

FRIZZLED BEEF IN BROWN MILK GRAVY

(Serves 4)

2 tablespoons butter	*3 tablespoons flour*
¼ pound sliced dried	*2 cups milk*
beef	*dash of pepper*

Melt the butter in a frying pan. Add the dried beef (shredded) and sauté lightly. Sprinkle the flour over the dried beef and brown until almost burnt, stirring all the while. Slowly add the milk and stir until the mixture boils. Add pepper.

If thicker than desired, stir in an additional ½ cup milk. Serve on toast or mashed potatoes.

BEEF CROQUETTES

(Serves 6 to 8)

Did you ever buy a beef roast in anticipation of the leftover beef so you could make croquettes? I much prefer them made with gravy than white sauce. Any amount of meat can be used in the proportion of ¼ cup of gravy for each cup of meat.

*3 cups ground leftover
  beef*
½ teaspoon salt
¾ cup gravy
*1 tablespoon minced
  onion*

1 cup dried breadcrumbs
1 egg
3 tablespoons water
shortening

Mix together the beef, salt, gravy, and onion. Chill for several hours so that you can shape croquettes easily. To coat: roll croquettes in breadcrumbs, then dip into the liquid (3 tablespoons water added to slightly beaten egg). Fry in a generous amount of shortening.

HAMBURG BALLS

(Serves 4 to 6)

The addition of bread or potatoes makes a world of difference to meat balls—a flavorful texture change.

1 egg
2 slices bread
¼ cup milk
*1 pound lean ground
  beef*
*2 tablespoons chopped
  onion*

salt and pepper
flour
*2 tablespoons bacon
  fat or vegetable
  shortening*

Break the egg into a quart-size bowl and beat slightly. Into this break up the bread into tiny pieces. Stir in the milk. Add the meat, onion, salt, and pepper. Mix thoroughly and shape into 6 patties, each an inch thick. Whenever mixture gets too wet to shape nicely, several tablespoons of dried breadcrumbs can be added. Roll in flour and fry in shortening in covered skillet for 20 to 30 minutes.

VARIATIONS:

Whenever you have leftover mashed potatoes, use about ½ cup in place of the bread.

Leftover gravy gives added flavor and nourishment, so use it when you can, in place of the milk.

BEEF LIVER STEW

(Serves 4)

2 onions	3 potatoes
¼ cup vegetable shortening	2 carrots
	1 teaspoon salt
1 pound beef liver	1½ cups water
2 tablespoons flour	salt and pepper

Slice onions and brown in shortening. When they begin to brown, push to one side and add liver that has been rolled in flour. When it is well browned, reduce heat and simmer for 20 minutes.

Meanwhile, cook quartered potatoes and sliced carrots with 1 teaspoon salt in 1½ cups water for 15 minutes. Season liver to taste. Add potatoes and carrots to liver and simmer all together for another 10 minutes.

STUFFED BEEF HEART

(Serves 6)

1 beef heart	*2 tablespoons butter*
2 tablespoons minced onion	*1 egg, beaten*
2 tablespoons celery, cut fine	*2 tablespoons water*
	1½ cups bread cubes
	salt and pepper

Soak beef heart in cold water for 2 hours. Drain. Remove veins, arteries, and muscles. Parboil for 20 minutes and remove from liquid to cool.

Sauté onion and celery in melted butter for 5 minutes over low heat. Combine beaten egg, water, bread cubes, and salt and pepper to taste. Mix well. Stuff cooled heart with bread filling. Cover opening with clean muslin and secure with skewers. Bake in covered roaster for 3 hours at 325°. Add hot water if needed.

WIENER SCHNITZEL

(*Breaded Veal Cutlets*)

(Serves 6)

1½ pounds veal steak, cut thin	*vegetable shortening*
2 eggs	*paprika, salt, and pepper*
¼ cup water	*ketchup*
1½ cups dried breadcrumbs	

With kitchen shears cut veal into serving pieces. In a soup plate lightly beat the eggs with a fork. Add the water and beat again. Bread each slice of meat by dipping into the egg mixture, then into crumbs, and patting well. Repeat dipping into the eggs and crumbs. Chill for ½ hour or more.

Fry in vegetable shortening over medium heat sprinkling with paprika, salt, and pepper. Fry until brown on both sides. Continue cooking over low heat until meat is tender (about 30 minutes), with skillet tightly covered until last 5 minutes. Serve with ketchup.

HAM LOAF

(Serves 6)

You may utilize leftover ham, and the dish is good enough for any guest.

3 cups minced cooked ham	¼ teaspoon pepper
1 small onion	1 tablespoon prepared mustard
1 teaspoon dried parsley	½ cup dried breadcrumbs
2 eggs, well beaten	1 cup milk

Put cooked ham and onion through food chopper. Add remaining ingredients and beat well. Pack into greased loaf pan 10×2 inches. Bake 40 minutes in a 350° oven.

SCHNITZ UN KNEPP

(*Dried Apple Slices and Dumplings*)

(Serves 6 to 8)

Sweet apples are *schnitzed* (sliced) and dried for this winter favorite of schnitz cooked with ham and dumplings, always known as Schnitz un Knepp.

The natives of Lehigh and Carbon counties like to be different. They are the only people in all of the Pennsylvania Dutch Country who serve Schnitz un Knepp with milk poured over it. Each man to his own liking!

2 *cups dried sweet apples*	½ *teaspoon salt*
2 *pounds smoked ham*	1 *egg, beaten*
2 *tablespoons brown sugar*	2 *tablespoons melted butter*
2 *cups flour*	⅔ *cup milk, approximately*
4 *teaspoons baking powder*	

Cover the dried apples with water and soak overnight. In the morning, using a large kettle, cover the ham with cold water and cook slowly for 2 hours. Add the apples and the water in which they were soaked. Add brown sugar and cook 1 hour longer.

Make the *knepp* by sifting together the flour, baking powder, and salt. Stir in beaten egg and melted butter. Add enough milk to make a moderately stiff dough. Drop from spoon into boiling ham and apples. Cook, without lifting the lid, for 20 minutes.

PORK, SAUERKRAUT, AND DUMPLINGS

(Serves 8)

When a wave of patriotic fervor swept the country in 1917–18, sauerkraut had to be disguised under the name of Liberty Cabbage!

Although many Pennsylvania Dutch cooks make their own sauerkraut or buy it by the pound from their butchers, canned sauerkraut is listed in this recipe. If you made your own, so much the better. Use a quart of it. Some cooks like to boil enough sauerkraut for two meals, serving mashed potatoes with it the first day and dumplings with it the second.

3-pound piece of	*1 teaspoon baking*
pork loin	*powder*
2 teaspoons salt	*¼ teaspoon salt*
1 large can sauerkraut	*1 egg, beaten*
1½ cups sifted flour	*¼ cup milk*

Put pork loin in a large kettle with enough water to cover. Simmer for 2 hours. Add salt and sauerkraut to pork and cook for another hour. During last half hour of cooking, mix up dumplings: Sift together the flour, baking powder, and salt. Add the beaten egg, stirring into the flour with a fork. Add milk and mix thoroughly.

Drop dumplings by spoonfuls onto boiling kraut (not into liquid). Cover tightly and let steam for 20 minutes without lifting lid.

HOT HORSE-RADISH SAUCE

(1 cup)

A delicious relish for beef and pork. It is also used over asparagus and spinach.

½ cup grated	*½ cup milk or cream*
horse-radish	*1 teaspoon butter*
1 teaspoon flour	*yolk of 1 egg*

Combine all ingredients in a saucepan. Beat well with a fork. Cook over low heat, stirring constantly, just until the mixture boils freely. Serve at once, or serve cold if you prefer.

POTATO FILLING, CABBAGE, AND SAUSAGE

(Serves 6)

Potato Filling*   1 small head cabbage
4 potatoes   1 pound sausage
1 teaspoon salt

Prepare Potato Filling and set aside.

Peel and slice 4 more potatoes and put into a large kettle. Add salt and water to almost cover. Heat. When almost boiling, cover with wedges of cabbage.

Over the cabbage, on the outside edge, put sausage. Fill center of sausage ring with Potato Filling. Cover and boil for 30 minutes.

STUFFED PORK CHOPS

(Serves 4)

This recipe is easily adjusted for any number of people. For each double chop use 1 slice of bread and ½ tablespoon each of butter, onion, celery, and water.

2 tablespoons minced   salt and pepper to
  onion   taste
2 tablespoons minced   4 slices bread
  celery   4 double-rib pork
2 tablespoons butter   chops with pocket
2 tablespoons water   ½ cup water

Sauté onion and celery in butter for 5 minutes. Remove from heat. Add to this the water, salt and pepper to taste. Combine with bread that has been broken into fine crumbs. Stuff into pork chops and secure with toothpicks. Sear in greased hot skillet over high heat to brown chops. When browned, place on rack in roast pan with ½ cup water and bake 1 hour at 350°, turning once during baking. Remove toothpicks before serving.

HOG MAW

(*Stuffed Pig Stomach*)

(Serves 8 to 10)

8 *large potatoes*	1 *tablespoon salt*
1 *pound fresh*	1 *pig stomach*
sausage meat	¼ *cup water*

Peel potatoes and dice into ½-inch cubes. Mix with sausage meat and salt. Stuff into pig stomach and sew the opening. Place in a roast pan with ¼ cup water. Cover and bake for 3 hours at 300°. Uncover for the last 30 minutes.

SQUIRREL POTPIE

(Serves 6)

1 *squirrel*	1 *tablespoon minced*
Potpie* dough	*parsley*
1 *large potato,*	½ *cup flour*
peeled and sliced	3 *tablespoons butter*
salt and pepper	1 *cup water*

Boil the squirrel until tender. Remove from broth.
Prepare Potpie dough squares. Drop into broth the peeled and sliced potato, 2 teaspoons salt, ¼ teaspoon pepper, and

parsley. Drop in the dough squares also. Cover and boil for 20 minutes.

Roll pieces of squirrel in flour, then brown in the butter. After removing squirrel from skillet, pour the water in the skillet, then add this same water to potpie before serving.

SCRAPPLE I

(10 servings)

Adapted for preparation in your own kitchen. Easier than you think!

3 pounds spareribs	*1 teaspoon dried*
3½ cups beef broth	*parsley*
(2 14-ounce cans)	*2 bay leaves*
1 teaspoon salt	*2 cups water*
⅛ teaspoon black	*2½ cups corn meal*
pepper	*flour*
1 medium onion,	*shortening*
chopped fine	

Cook spareribs in beef broth in which salt, pepper, onion, parsley, and bay leaves have been added. Simmer for 2½ hours. Remove meat from broth and strain broth. Cut meat from bone and gristle. Put meat through food chopper. Return to broth and bring to a boil.

Slowly add water to corn meal while stirring. Add some of the hot broth too. Pour corn meal mixture into boiling broth and cook until very thick (about 10 minutes). Pour into 2 loaf pans, 9×5×3 inches. Chill.

When cold, cut into ½-inch slices and coat with flour before frying. Fry in very little shortening until outside is very brown and crisp.

SCRAPPLE II

(*Pawnhaas*)

Butchering days are great days on the farm. Somehow this butchering process has a way of involving the whole family. While the menfolks start slaughtering, the farm wife is scurrying hither and yon setting up the tubs and crocks on the long benches. She has everything scoured and in readiness when the first tubs of meat are brought in. From here on the kitchen buzzes with activity.

To cut up the roasts and steaks is one operation, but to tackle the task of making the bologna, sausage, pudding, and scrapple starts a processing routine. Later the hams, bacon, and sausage will be hung in the smokehouse where they will be cured.

One of the most important operations at butchering time is the making of scrapple. It is made as follows:

3 quarts broth	*2 teaspoons salt*
2 cups cooked pork	*½ teaspoon pepper*
meat, cut fine	*½ teaspoon sage,*
3 cups corn meal	*if desired*

Make the broth by boiling together one cleaned hog's head with heart and liver and pieces of pork. Cook several hours. Remove the meat from the bones and measure. What is left can be used in making meat pudding.

Bring the meat and broth to a boil. Into it dribble the corn meal, stirring constantly until the consistency of mush has been achieved. Add seasonings and cook slowly for an hour. Pour into loaf pans, 9×5×3 inches, and cool. Slice and fry when cold.

BUCKWHEAT SCRAPPLE

Prepared as above, but ⅓ cup buckwheat is substituted for ⅓ cup of the corn meal.

HOMEMADE BOLOGNA

Here is a recipe that I did not test and probably never shall. Having had requests for recipes for home butchering, I asked my neighbor for help. Her father went from farm to farm to do butchering and this was his recipe. Soon after I published it, a reader in California used it with great success to make bologna with deer meat! She even sent me a sample!

50 pounds beef
10 pounds pork
1½ ounces mace
1¼ quarts salt
5 ounces black pepper

1 ounce cloves
4 pounds brown sugar
2½ ounces saltpeter
dissolved in warm
water

"Make bags from new muslin. With seams on outside, fill with bologna mixture. Smoke."

Why the saltpeter? That keeps the color red!

SOUSE

(*Jellied Pig's Feet*)

Pennsylvania Dutch people also speak of this by names of *Tzitterli*, *Sultz*, and *Gallerich*. Some like a sour souse and add vinegar to the brine. Each cook seems to have her own variation, some adding a bit of veal and others flavoring with cloves and cinnamon.

Boil 2 pig's feet with tongue of pig until meat falls off the bones. Discard bones, gristle, and skin. Cut meat very fine and divide into custard cups. Bring broth to a full boil, seasoning with salt and pepper, then pour over meat. Stir and cool. To serve, unmold and slice.

OYSTER POTPIE

(Serves 6)

If you prefer, you can omit the bottom crust.

3 potatoes, diced
1 carrot, diced
2 stems celery, diced
1 cup water
½ teaspoon salt
2 tablespoons butter
2 tablespoons flour
½ teaspoon salt
1 cup milk
Pastry for Two-Crust
* Pie**

1 cup stewing oysters
(about 15)
1 tablespoon minced
* onion*
1 tablespoon minced
* parsley*
2 hard-cooked eggs,
* sliced*
black pepper

Cook potatoes, carrot, and celery in 1 cup water with the ½ teaspoon salt for 20 minutes.

Melt butter, remove from heat, and stir in 2 tablespoons flour and salt. Blend in the milk and cook until thick, stirring constantly. Combine with cooked drained vegetables.

Turn half of this mixture into pastry-lined pie plate. Cover with oysters, onion, parsley, and hard-cooked eggs. Season with black pepper. Add remaining sauce and potatoes. Cover with pastry. Bake 20 minutes at 425°.

OYSTER PIE

(Serves 6 to 8)

Oysterhouses are landmarks in our cities. Oysters were featured both to be eaten there in the oyster parlor and to be taken out for home cooking. Today the little oyster parlors are being replaced with seafood restaurants that serve great varieties of seafood and fresh-water fish with full-course Pennsylvania Dutch dinners.

This deep-dish Oyster Pie is a traditional festive dish served at Thanksgiving, Christmas, and New Year.

Pastry for Two-Crust	*3 stems celery, cut fine*
Pie*	*3 tablespoons butter*
1 pint stewing oysters	*1 teaspoon salt*
3 cups crushed Trenton	*¼ teaspoon pepper*
oyster crackers	*1½ cups milk*

Line a 2-quart casserole with the pastry. Put in alternate layers of oysters, crushed crackers, celery, butter, and seasonings. Add the milk. Cover with top pastry, cutting slits in it to let out steam. Bake in a 375° oven for 45 minutes.

OYSTER CORN PIE

(Serves 6)

This used to be a September treat when fresh corn was available. Oysters tasted especially good too. We never ate oysters in summertime. Grandma insisted that one only ate oysters in the months that had an *r* in them. So—no one ate oysters in May, June, or July.

Pastry for Two-Crust
 9-inch Pie*
2 cups fresh corn,
 cut from the cob
½ cup milk
1 tablespoon butter
1 teaspoon salt

1 teaspoon sugar
1 tablespoon chopped
 parsley
2 hard-cooked eggs,
 sliced
½ dozen stewing oysters

Line a 9-inch piepan with pastry. Heat the corn with the milk and butter. Put half of corn into pastry. Add seasonings, eggs, and oysters. Cover with remaining corn, then top pastry. Prick with fork. Bake 10 minutes in a very hot oven, 400°. Reduce heat to 325° and bake 35 minutes longer. Serve hot.

SCALLOPED OYSTERS

(Serves 6)

This excellent oyster dish is served with chicken or turkey dinners.

¼ pound crispy
 saltines
1 cup stewing oysters
salt and pepper

¼ cup celery, cut fine
2 tablespoons butter
1½ cups hot milk

In a buttered casserole arrange layers of saltines, oysters, salt and pepper, celery, and butter, topping with crackers. Cover with hot milk. Cover casserole and bake for 30 minutes in a 350° oven.

DEVILED CLAMS

(Serves 8)

Thirty years ago in my home town of Lititz, Lancaster County, this delicacy was a regular item for Saturday night's supper. The deviled clams were bought already prepared from a family that took orders for them and then delivered them in a big chip basket that was covered with blue and white checked oilcloth. What a pity that no one takes orders for them any more!

12 clams
2 medium onions
½ loaf bread,
  crumbled
3 hard-cooked eggs,
  chopped
1 tablespoon minced
  parsley

dash of Worcestershire
  sauce
1 egg, beaten
1 tablespoon butter,
  browned
clam juice
¼ cup dry breadcrumbs

Wash clams thoroughly and put through the food chopper with the onions. Add the pieces of bread, chopped eggs, and parsley and mix thoroughly.

Combine the Worcestershire sauce, beaten egg, and browned butter. Combine both mixtures and moisten with clam juice if necessary.

Fill buttered seafood shells and refrigerate for 1 day. Sprinkle dry breadcrumbs over the top. Fry in hot shortening with shells upside down. Fry only until nicely browned.

BAKED SHAD

(Serves 6)

No marinade needed, we say. Plain shad is good enough for us.

3 pounds shad	*2 tablespoons cream,*
½ teaspoon salt	*heated*
1 tablespoon browned	*2 tablespoons chopped*
butter	*parsley*

Place shad in roaster and salt. (No need to bone shad if prepared this way. Long baking makes bones edible.) Half-cover with water and bake uncovered in a 350° oven for 3 hours. To serve, place on serving platter and pour browned butter and cream over it. Sprinkle with chopped parsley.

SCHMIERKASE

(Pennsylvania Dutch Cottage Cheese)

Put a quart of milk into an earthen crock and keep in a warm place until it thickens. Put into a cheesecloth bag and hang up to drain. It should drain for at least a day.

To the dry curds left in the bag, slowly add an equal amount of light cream, working it in until the cheese has a creamy consistency and is soft enough to spread on apple-butter bread. Add salt to suit your taste.

EGG CHEESE

(2 heart molds)

2 quarts milk	*4 eggs, beaten*
2 tablespoons cornstarch	*2½ cups buttermilk*

Heat milk, except ¼ cup. Mix this ¼ cup milk with the cornstarch. When cornstarch and milk have been mixed to a smooth paste, stir it into the 4 beaten eggs. To this add the buttermilk.

When the heated milk is almost boiling, pour the egg and buttermilk mixture into it. Allow this to simmer over low heat for 45 minutes, stirring frequently to prevent scorching. Pour into 2 cheese molds and let drain for several hours. Chill before serving.

Potatoes

THREE times a day, for breakfast, dinner, and supper, the Pennsylvania Dutch used to eat potatoes. In rural areas it is still a regular custom, but in urban parts it is only an occasional practice. In past generations, when everybody had potatoes three meals each day, a double quantity of potatoes was regularly cooked so there would be leftovers to fry for the next meal. Today, at noon, it is not unusual to find both white potatoes and sweet potatoes on the dinner table—perhaps noodles, too. Potatoes that are left over one day are fried for the next breakfast.

The utilization of leftovers is interesting. There is a great variety of potato cakes—pan-fried and deep-fat-fried. The combination of potatoes and bread is endless, each cook using proportions to suit her own special liking. It makes no difference whether the leftovers are boiled or mashed potatoes, we have numerous ways of using each.

The Pennsylvania Dutch have always excelled in budget control and the cooks surely demonstrate this in their potato cookery. However, they serve potatoes every meal for appetite appeal as well as for economic reasons. After all, they know very well that a meal needs to have a starch in it if it is to be completely satisfying.

POTATO CAKES I

(Serves 4 to 6)

1 cup mashed potatoes
1 egg
6 tablespoons flour
½ teaspoon baking powder

1 teaspoon salt
¼ cup milk
2 tablespoons lard or other shortening

Mix all ingredients, except lard, in the order given. Drop from tablespoon into hot lard that has been melted in a skillet. When cakes are rather well set and brown around the edges, turn and brown on other side. It may be necessary to add more lard if the skillet becomes dry.

POTATO CAKES II

(Serves 6)

2 cups leftover mashed potatoes
1 small onion, minced

1 slice bread
1 egg, beaten
vegetable shortening

To the mashed potatoes, add onion and bread that has been pulled into small pieces. Mix well. Shape into 6 thick cakes. Dip into beaten egg and fry in hot vegetable shortening (just about 3 tablespoons shortening needed).

POTATO CAKES III

(German style)

(Serves 4)

2 eggs	*2 tablespoons flour*
2 cups grated raw	*1 teaspoon scraped*
potato	*onion*
1 teaspoon salt	*bacon fat or lard*

Beat the eggs and add the potato and salt. Mix thoroughly, then stir in the flour and onion. Drop from tablespoon into hot bacon fat. Brown on both sides.

SCALLOPED POTATOES

(Serves 6)

It's saffron that makes the scalloped potatoes so flavorful and colorful.

4 medium potatoes	*2 tablespoons flour*
1 teaspoon salt	*2 tablespoons butter*
pepper to taste	*1 cup milk*
1 teaspoon saffron	*1 cup cream*

Peel and slice potatoes very thin. Mix together salt, pepper, saffron, and flour.

Butter a 1½-quart covered baking dish. Fill it with layers

of potatoes. On each layer, except the top one, put some of the seasoned flour and bits of butter. Mix milk and cream together and pour over potatoes. Cover and bake in a 300° oven for 1 hour.

SCALLOPED POTATOES WITH CRAB

(Serves 4)

4 medium potatoes	*¼ cup chopped onion*
salt and pepper to taste	*1 cup crab meat*
4 teaspoons flour	*2 cups milk*

Pare potatoes and slice 2 of them into buttered casserole. Sprinkle with salt, pepper, and 2 teaspoons flour. Cover with 2 tablespoons onion and ½ cup crab. Make another layer of sliced potatoes, seasonings, onion, and crab. Heat milk and pour over the top. Bake, covered, for an hour in 350° oven.

POTATO BALLS, DEEP-FRIED

(Serves 4 to 5)

One of the very best uses for leftover mashed potatoes. A recipe that should be in every kitchen.

1 cup mashed potatoes	*1 teaspoon salt*
1 cup flour, unsifted	*1 egg, well beaten*
1 teaspoon baking powder	*5 tablespoons milk*

Mix the ingredients in the order given. Fry in deep fat, dropping from a tablespoon. Fat is hot enough when a cube of bread browns in 1 minute (350°). When potato balls are brown, drain on paper towels. Serve hot.

FRIED POTATOES WITH EGGS

(Serves 6)

What a good supper dish this is! Also good for breakfast.

2 cups leftover boiled
  potatoes
2 tablespoons lard or
  vegetable shortening

3 eggs
salt and pepper to taste

Slice the cold leftover potatoes. Fry in hot lard that has been melted in the skillet. When potatoes are nicely browned, break the eggs over them, stirring quickly through the potatoes. Sprinkle with salt and pepper. Fry a few minutes longer until the eggs are cooked.

HOT POTATO SALAD

(Serves 4)

Because of its name, this one was almost put into the salad chapter. It is served as a vegetable, so it belongs here with the other potato dishes.

2 cups diced potatoes
2 slices bacon
¼ cup chopped onion
¼ cup chopped green
  pepper
1 egg

2 tablespoons vinegar
½ teaspoon salt
⅛ teaspoon pepper
1 teaspoon sugar
2 hard-cooked eggs,
  sliced

Cook the potatoes in salted water. (Freshly boiled hot potatoes are needed for this dish, so do not use leftover potatoes.)

Dice bacon and fry. When partly fried, add onion and green pepper. Sauté 3 minutes.

Beat the egg and add to it the vinegar, salt, pepper, and sugar. Add to the bacon mixture in the frying pan and cook over medium heat, stirring, until mixture thickens.

Drain the cooked potatoes and combine with the sauce and 1 sliced hard-cooked egg. Serve with other egg sliced over the top.

POTATO FILLING I

(Serves 6)

One of the most interesting of all Pennsylvania Dutch dishes is the Potato Filling. It is an elaboration of mashed potatoes, made by beating bread cubes, onion, and celery into ordinary mashed potatoes. It was an ingenious Pennsylvania Dutch cook who discovered this delicious combination of bread and potatoes.

4 large potatoes	½ teaspoon salt
1 onion	pepper to taste
2 tablespoons butter	hot milk, about 1 cup
3 slices bread, cubed	or
3 tablespoons chopped parsley	part hot milk and part chicken broth
3 tablespoons chopped celery leaves	1 beaten egg
	2 tablespoons butter

Peel potatoes and cut into eighths. Cook in salted water. Meanwhile, in a skillet sauté onion in butter. When onion is beginning to brown, add bread cubes and brown them too.

When potatoes are soft, drain and mash. Add bread mixture, parsley, celery leaves, salt, and pepper. Adding hot milk gradually, or part hot milk and part chicken broth, beat all together with electric mixer. (Chicken broth substituted for some of the milk will give added flavor. Chicken giblets, chopped fine are a good addition too.)

Add beaten egg and beat until mixture is well blended. Turn into a greased baking dish. Dot with butter. Bake 30 minutes in a 350° oven.

POTATO FILLING II

(Serves 6)

No one can imagine the goodness of this combination until he tries it.

4 potatoes
4 slices bread
1 cup milk
¼ cup diced onion
2 tablespoons minced
celery

3 tablespoons butter
1 teaspoon salt
dash of pepper

Peel the potatoes, cut into pieces, and cook in salted water. Drain and mash. Break the bread into pieces and mix with the potatoes. Heat milk, then beat into potatoes and bread.

Sauté onion and celery in butter for 3 minutes. Add to potatoes with salt, and pepper. Beat with beater until well mixed. Put into greased casserole and bake for 45 minutes in 350° oven.

PIGEONS

(*Potato Dumplings*)

(4 large dumplings)

The category of Potato Dumplings is complicated. This is partially true because each cook has her own favorite fillings for the dumplings and also because each family had adopted its own names for the dish. And what names they are! The following are names for potato dumplings: Old Shoes,* Filled Noodles,* Pants Pockets, Pigeons,* Potato *Knepp, Fillich Knepp* (Filled Dumpling), and Boova Shenkel* (Boy's Thighs). The dumplings are made with biscuit dough or noodle dough and filled with either mashed potatoes, fried potatoes, boiled potatoes, or Potato Filling.*

4 *potatoes*	1 *hard-cooked egg,*
3 *cups flour*	*chopped*
1 *teaspoon salt*	1 *grated onion*
3 *teaspoons baking*	1 *tablespoon chopped*
powder	*parsley*
3 *tablespoons butter*	2 *tablespoons butter*
¾ *cup water*	*hot milk*

Cook pared, quartered potatoes in salt water until soft. Meanwhile, sift together the flour, salt, and baking powder. Cut the butter into the dry ingredients with two knives. Make a well in the center of these ingredients and pour the water into it. Stir cautiously until there is no danger of spilling it, then stir vigorously. Roll out ¼ of the dough into an 8-inch round.

When the potatoes are soft, drain them and combine with egg, onion, and parsley. Put ¼ of the potatoes on each dumpling round. Fold over to make half-moon pies, pressing edges together firmly. Steam over boiling water for 25 minutes.

To serve: Place dumplings in soup plates. Melt butter in hot milk and pour over dumplings.

Note: For an extra-special dish, prepare Oyster Stew* with minced oysters and serve over Pigeon dumplings.

POTATO PIE

(Serves 6)

*Pastry for Two-Crust
Pie**
*4 large potatoes, peeled
and sliced*
1 teaspoon salt
*⅛ teaspoon black
pepper*

1 small onion, minced
*1 teaspoon dried
parsley*
2 teaspoons flour
¼ cup cream

Line a 9-inch pie plate with pastry. Fill with slices of peeled
raw potatoes. Sprinkle with seasonings, onion, parsley, and flour.
Pour cream over top. Cover with top crust, putting slits in the
top to let steam escape. Bake for 1 hour in a 350° oven.

OLD SHOES

(*Potato Dumplings*)

(4 large dumplings)

The Pennsylvania Dutchman says, "Them that work hard,
eat hearty." That they do. This is the kind of food that gives
you that long-satisfied feeling.

3 large potatoes
3 cups flour
1 teaspoon salt
*5 teaspoons baking
powder*
*⅓ cup vegetable
shortening*
¾ cup milk

1 tablespoon butter
⅓ cup milk
4 tablespoons butter
*1 tablespoon minced
parsley or 1 teaspoon
dried parsley*
black pepper
milk

Peel and cut potatoes and cook in salted water until soft. Meanwhile, make biscuit dough by sifting the flour, salt, and baking powder together, then cutting in the shortening and moistening with milk. Turn dough out on floured board and knead for 5 or 6 turns. Take ¼ of dough and roll into a 10-inch round.

When potatoes are soft, drain. Mash with butter and ⅓ cup milk. Bring 3 quarts hot water to a boil in a deep kettle. (An old plate should be placed in the bottom of the kettle to keep dumplings from sticking to the bottom.) Put ¼ of mashed potatoes onto dough. Lift edges of dough to enclose potatoes, pinching together at top as you would for apple dumplings. Drop into the kettle of boiling water and boil for 20 minutes.

After 20 minutes melt the 4 tablespoons butter in a skillet over medium heat and place dumplings in skillet. Sprinkle them with parsley and pepper. When dumplings are nicely browned, serve in soup plates with milk.

FILLED NOODLES

(4 large dumplings)

This kind of dumpling has boiled potatoes combined with egg and wrapped in a noodle dough.

4 potatoes	1 egg, beaten
2 eggs	salt and pepper
2 cups sifted flour	2 cups milk
1 tablespoon water	8 slices bacon, diced
¼ teaspoon salt	and fried

Cook pared and quartered potatoes until soft. Make noodle dough by mixing the eggs, flour, water, and salt. Knead with fingers until well mixed. Roll out ¼ of the dough at a time into 8-inch rounds.

When potatoes are soft, drain, then combine with beaten egg. Add salt and pepper (to taste) and mix well. Place ¼ of potato mixture on each round of dough. Bring opposite ends of dough together and press firmly together. It is a good idea to moisten edges of dough before enclosing dumplings.

Drop into 3 quarts of boiling water and cook for 20 minutes. Serve with hot milk into which you have put diced and fried bacon.

BOOVA SHENKEL

(*Potato Dumplings*)

(Serves 6)

Boova Shenkel, translated, means "Boy's Thighs," which seems utterly strange for these potato dumplings. But then, similar dumplings also have strange names, like "Pants Pockets" and "Old Shoes."

1½ to 2 pounds lean boiling beef	*4 potatoes*
	salt and pepper
2 cups flour	*2 eggs*
2 teaspoons baking powder	*2 tablespoons butter*
	1 onion, minced
1 tablespoon lard	*1 tablespoon minced parsley*
1 tablespoon butter	
½ cup water	*4 tablespoons butter*

Stew the beef for about 2 hours, or until tender. During the last hour, prepare the dumpling dough as follows:

Sift together the flour and baking powder. Cut in the lard

and butter and slowly add water, stirring lightly. Roll into 6 circles, 8 inches in diameter. Set aside.

Pare potatoes and slice thin. Season to taste with salt and pepper. Add enough water to barely cover and cook until tender. When soft, combine with 2 eggs (beaten), butter, onion, and parsley. Let stand for 10 minutes. Divide mixture and spread on dough circles. Then wet the dough edges and fold in half to form half-moons. Seal edges.

Drop into broth to cook with meat for 30 minutes. Lift from broth and brown in a skillet using the 4 tablespoons butter. Serve hot with beef.

SWEET POTATO CROQUETTES

(Serves 6)

So nice to serve to guests, and can be prepared a day ahead.

2 cups mashed sweet potatoes (about 6)	1 egg, unbeaten
	1 tablespoon water
1 teaspoon salt	½ cup dried breadcrumbs
2 tablespoons butter	¼ cup shortening
1 egg, beaten	

To the mashed sweet potatoes add the salt, butter, and beaten egg. Chill for 4 hours or longer.

Shape into croquettes. For coating: Break egg into a soup dish and beat slightly with a fork; then add the tablespoon of water. Dip croquettes in crumbs and pat crumbs all over croquettes. Roll in beaten egg and into crumbs again. If time allows, chill again in refrigerator, as croquettes hold their shape best if chilled before frying. Pan-fry in shortening.

Vegetables

In the Garden Spot of America, as the Pennsylvania Dutch Country has long been called, vegetables are at their best. The rich soil and the tender loving care of the Pennsylvania Dutch farmers and gardeners produce first-rate vegetables. To the cooks, freshness is of vital importance, and they insist on it. To get a vegetable from the garden to the pot in just thirty minutes is their aim. That is the secret of the goodness of Pennsylvania Dutch vegetable cookery. Beginning with leaf lettuce in the early spring, these fresh vegetables are enjoyed until the last celery and turnips are gathered. The produce huckster understands this demand for freshness too. How well I remember the corn huckster who passed our house with his horse and wagon, calling out loud and clear: "Just picked this morning!" Among the Pennsylvania Dutch there is an excellent philosophy that demands using what one has to the very best advantage. Very little produce is wasted. Some excellent vegetable recipes were created to utilize the sudden garden abundance.

The uninhibited use of butter is the one extravagance of Pennsylvania Dutch cooks, and it is evident in their vegetable cookery. Another important ingredient is sugar. They like sugar, and cooks generally season vegetables with equal parts of salt and sugar. Even vegetable soup is sometimes sweetened.

Boiled dinners are extremely popular. Green beans or cabbage, boiled with potatoes and ham, is a common dish in every home. Succulent pies are made with either corn, onions, or potatoes, and served piping hot. The greatest variety in preparation is found in corn and cabbage. Corn is stewed, baked, scalloped, and fried, and cabbage is boiled, stuffed, soured, and fried. Even though herbs are used sparingly, there is no monotony in vegetable cookery. Other vegetables that are grown and used here are squash, Lima beans, eggplant, salsify, asparagus, beets, broccoli, Brussels sprouts, peas, carrots, tomatoes, cauliflower, spinach, and parsnips. All of these are served as buttered vegetables, but only the unusual ways of serving that are peculiar to this cookery are given in this chapter.

PENNSYLVANIA DUTCH CABBAGE

(Serves 6)

In this regional cookery, cabbage and vinegar seem to be inseparable. Vinegar is used not only in the coleslaw, but in hot dishes like this one.

5 cups shredded cabbage
4 slices bacon, diced
2 tablespoons brown
  sugar
2 tablespoons flour

½ cup water
⅓ cup vinegar
salt and pepper
1 small onion, minced

Cook cabbage in 2 quarts salted boiling water for 7 minutes. Fry bacon pieces and set aside. To the bacon fat add the sugar and flour and blend. Add the water, vinegar, and seasonings to taste. Cook until thickened.

Add the sweet-sour sauce with the onion and bacon to the cooked drained cabbage. Heat thoroughly and serve.

STEAMED CABBAGE AND POTATOES

(Serves 6)

2 tablespoons bacon fat
1 medium-size head
  cabbage, cut into
  8 chunks

6 medium potatoes,
  pared and sliced
2 teaspoons salt
⅛ teaspoon pepper
½ cup boiling water

Melt bacon fat in a 9-inch skillet. Add cabbage, potatoes, and seasonings. Pour the boiling water over it. Cover skillet and steam very slowly for 40 minutes.

STUFFED CABBAGE

(Serves 6 to 8)

Nice to serve with Meat Loaf.* 'Tis almost a meal in itself.

1 small head cabbage
2 teaspoons salt
Bread Filling* (ready
  for baking)

2 slices bread, buttered
2 tablespoons butter

Cut out the heart of the cabbage and cook in a deep kettle with the salt and enough water to cover it. Cook for 45 minutes or until tender. Prepare Bread Filling.

Place cooked cabbage in buttered casserole, then put Bread Filling between the cabbage leaves. Top with bread that has been cubed and browned in butter. Cover and bake for 45 minutes at 350°.

DUTCH BEANS

(Serves 5 to 6)

To the Pennsylvania Dutch, green beans need vinegar. If vinegar isn't added by the cook, the vinegar cruet will be on the table.

1 pound green beans　　　*1 large onion, diced*
½ teaspoon savory　　　*⅓ cup vinegar*
*　 (optional)*　　　　　 *½ cup water*
4 slices bacon　　　　　*2 tablespoons sugar*

Cook the beans in salted water with the savory until tender, about 30 minutes. Dice bacon and fry with diced onion. When bacon is brown, add vinegar, water, and sugar. Pour over cooked drained beans.

DRIED STRING BEANS WITH HAM

The mention of this dish seems to give today's Pennsylvania Dutch a nostalgia for the "good old days." Just a very few still dry green beans.

Cook smoked ham. Meanwhile, soak dried beans in water for about an hour. Drain off the water and add the beans to the ham. Cook until almost tender, then add 1 potato for each person to be served. Cook until potatoes are soft. Serve with vinegar.

STUFFED PEPPERS

(6 medium peppers)

A most attractive vegetable garnish for meat platters. The tomato looks so gay when the peppers are cut in half.

6 green peppers
½ recipe for Bread
    Filling*
1 small onion, chopped
    fine

½ cup bits of leftover
    beef or pork
1 tomato, cut in little
    pieces

Remove tops from green peppers and take out all fiber and seeds. Scald 5 minutes in salted water.

Put peppers into greased baking dish and stuff with the prepared Bread Filling to which you have added the chopped onion, meat, and tomato.

Add ½ inch of water to peppers in baking dish. Cover with lid or foil. Bake peppers for 45 minutes at 350°. Cut peppers in half lengthwise to serve.

PEAS AND KNEPP (DUMPLINGS)

(Serves 4 to 6)

2 pounds green peas
    (2 cups hulled)
1 cup water
1 teaspoon sugar
½ teaspoon salt

2 tablespoons butter
¼ teaspoon salt
3 tablespoons flour
2 tablespoons water

Cook the peas in 1 cup water with sugar and salt about 20 minutes. Add just 1 tablespoon butter.

Crumble together the other tablespoon of butter with the salt and flour. Moisten with the water. Stir and beat until the mass forms a smooth ball. Drop tiny bits from a teaspoon (30 bits of *knepp*) into the peas. Cover and boil 5 minutes longer.

Note: Frozen peas may be used. A 10-ounce package equals 2 cups.

FRIED EGGPLANT

(Serves 6)

1 medium-size eggplant	½ cup vegetable
2 eggs	shortening
¼ cup water	tomato sauce or ketchup
2 cups dried	
breadcrumbs	

Pare the eggplant and cut into ¼-inch slices. Beat the eggs and add the water. Dip each slice of eggplant into the egg, then crumbs, patting the crumbs well onto the eggplant. Dip each slice into the egg and crumbs again. Fry in melted shortening until brown on both sides and tender. Serve with tomato sauce or ketchup.

FRIED PUMPKIN

(Serves 6)

Cut 12 slices, ¼ inch thick, from the peeled crook of a neck pumpkin. Prepare just like Fried Eggplant.*

SUGAR PEAS AND NEW POTATOES
(Serves 6)

When the Pennsylvania Dutch speak of sugar peas, they mean the kind with the edible pods. This is the vegetable that we consider "extra special." Favorite varieties have been kept within families for generations. In fact, the last picking is usually left on the stalk to dry, then pulled off later for next year's planting. For this succulent dish it is quite often necessary to search for the new potatoes. With trowel in hand, one hopefully goes to the garden, lifts the soil around potato stalks with care, and looks for potatoes that have attained the diameter of one inch! Of course, it's worth it.

*1 quart sugar peas with
    edible pods
14 tiny new potatoes
2 cups water
2 teaspoons salt*

*1 teaspoon sugar
1 cup milk or cream
2 tablespoons butter
(more if you like)*

String the washed sugar peas. (This is quickly done by cutting off the smallest end of the pod and pulling the string down the straight side. The other side can then be pulled from the blossom end. Scrub the potatoes well and pare, if you like—it is not necessary.

In one saucepan bring the peas and potatoes to a boil in 2 cups of water with salt and sugar added. Cook for 35 minutes. Add the milk or cream and butter. Keep over heat 1 minute more, then serve.

CORN PIE
(Serves 6)

2 cups fresh corn, cut
  from cob
about ½ cup milk or
  cream
1 tablespoon butter
1 teaspoon salt

1 teaspoon sugar
2 tablespoons chopped
  parsley or green
  pepper (optional)
Pastry for Two-Crust
  9-inch Pie*

Heat the corn with ¼ cup of the milk and then you can judge how much more milk you will need. If the corn itself does not have much liquid, you may even need more than the ½ cup. Add the butter and seasonings. Put into pastry-lined piepan. Cover with top crust. Prick with fork. Bake for 10 minutes in a very hot oven, 400°. Reduce heat to 325° and bake 35 minutes longer. Serve hot with the main course.

Note: For extra-special goodness, use grated fresh corn to make corn pie.

CORN PUDDING
(Serves 4 to 6)

6 ears (or 1 can
  cream-style) corn
1 tablespoon sugar
1 tablespoon cornstarch
1 teaspoon salt

3 eggs, beaten
  separately
4 tablespoons melted
  butter
1 cup milk

Combine all ingredients in the order given, except for the egg whites. Fold those in last. Place in a greased 1½-quart casserole and bake 35 minutes in a 350° oven.

FRIED CORN

(Serves 4)

4 slices bacon
2 cups fresh corn or
1 can ready-to-eat dried
corn

1 tablespoon minced
green pepper
1 tablespoon minced
red pepper

Fry bacon until crisp, then drain on paper towel. Discard all but 2 tablespoons of the fat. Add the corn and pepper. If using the canned corn, drain off liquid. Brown over hottest heat. When serving, crumble bacon over the top.

DRIED CORN

The oldest way of drying fruits and vegetables was by the heat of the summer sun. Today, one can still find a few who put trays of corn to dry out in the sun. Others use top-of-the-stove methods or dry it in the oven, as below. Also available today is the commercial dried corn packaged by John Cope Corn Co., East Petersburg, Pa. We may soon forget how Grandma used to put her dried corn in muslin bags and hang them in the attic.

Cook corn on the cob in boiling water for 3 minutes. Cut off and spread out in large pans that will fit in the oven. The broiler pan or roast pans are suitable. Dry in a very slow oven (200°), stirring every hour, for 5 to 6 hours, until thoroughly dry. Pack in sterilized jars and seal.

STEWED DRIED CORN
(Serves 4)

1 cup dried corn	*¼ teaspoon salt*
2 cups boiling water	*1 tablespoon sugar*
2 tablespoons milk	*2 tablespoons butter*

Cover corn with 2 cups boiling water and let soak for 2 hours. Add milk and seasonings and simmer for another hour. Add butter and serve.

SCALLOPED DRIED CORN
(Serves 6)

3 cups coarsely crushed	*3 tablespoons butter*
crispy crackers	*1 can ready-to-eat dried*
1 teaspoon salt	*corn*
⅛ teaspoon pepper	*2 cups milk*

Into a 2-quart buttered baking dish (with cover) put 1 cup of the crushed crackers. Sprinkle over these ½ teaspoon of salt and dash of pepper. Dot with 1 tablespoon butter. Cover with half the corn and another cup of crackers. Add remaining corn and seasonings. Cover with the last cup of crackers.

Pour milk over the whole and dot with remaining butter. Cover casserole and bake in a 375° oven for 35 minutes. Uncover and bake 10 minutes longer.

DRIED CORN PUDDING I
(Serves 6)

Dried Corn Pudding usually appears on the Thanksgiving Day menu, but it certainly is not limited to special occasions.

1 cup dried corn
2 cups hot milk
2 beaten eggs
2 tablespoons sugar

2 teaspoons salt
1 cup milk
1 tablespoon butter

Grind the dried corn in food chopper. Pour the hot milk over it and let stand an hour or longer.

To the soaked corn add beaten eggs, sugar, salt, and milk. Mix well, then pour into a greased baking dish 6×10×2 inches. Dot the top with butter. Bake 30 minutes (no longer) at 350°.

DRIED CORN PUDDING II

(Serves 8)

Very easy to make using canned evaporated corn that is ready to heat and serve.

3 eggs
2 15-ounce cans
  evaporated corn
1 cup milk

2 tablespoons butter,
  melted
2 teaspoons sugar

Beat the eggs in a medium-size bowl. To the eggs add the liquid you drain from the 2 cans of evaporated corn. Add the milk, melted butter, and sugar. Turn into a greased casserole and bake 45 minutes in a 350° oven.

SALTED CORN

A very old method for preserving corn, but seldom used today.

Cook corn on the cob for 5 minutes; then cut it off. To every quart of corn add a cup of salt. Mix well and pack in a crock. Cover and store in a cool place. To serve: Rinse and drain with hot water 4 times. Soak 5 hours before cooking. Stew until tender, then add sugar and cream as desired.

SCALLOPED OYSTER PLANT

(Baked Salsify Pudding)

(Serves 6)

There is not an oyster in the recipe, but it is a delicious vegetable casserole with oyster flavor.

6 roots of salsify	⅛ teaspoon pepper
3 cups slightly crushed saltines	3 tablespoons butter
	1½ cups milk
1 teaspoon salt	

Scrape salsify roots, cut into ½-inch slices, then parboil for 15 minutes. Drain.

Into a buttered casserole put alternate layers of crushed crackers, seasonings, butter, then salsify, having 3 layers of crackers and seasonings and 2 of salsify. Cover with the milk.

Bake, covered, for 45 minutes at 375°, uncovering casserole for last 15 minutes.

ONION PIE

(Serves 6)

Another pie that is served hot as a main dish.

Pastry for Pie Shell*	1 teaspoon salt
2 tablespoons flour	dash of pepper
8 or 9 onions, sliced	1 cup cream
2 tablespoons butter	2 slices bacon

Line an 8-inch piepan with pastry. Sprinkle flour over the pastry. Cover with sliced onions. Dot with butter and season with salt, and pepper. Pour cream over the top. Partially fry the diced bacon, then lay over onions. Bake 45 minutes in a 350° oven. Serve hot.

DUTCH TURNIPS

(Serves 6)

When the name "Dutch" is used with any vegetable dish, you can expect to find vinegar in the recipe. Making vegetables sour is a characteristic of Pennsylvania Dutch cookery.

8 turnips	*2 tablespoons vinegar*
2 cups water	*3 tablespoons butter*
1 teaspoon salt	

Peel turnips. Cut in thin slices and cook in 2 cups water with 1 teaspoon salt for 20 minutes. Drain. Add vinegar and butter.

SWEET AND SOUR CELERY

(Serves 4)

2 cups celery, cut	*2 tablespoons vinegar*
in 1-inch pieces	*3 tablespoons sugar*
2 cups water	*2 tablespoons butter*
½ teaspoon salt	

Cook celery in water with salt for 30 minutes. Drain, then add remaining ingredients. Serve hot. To serve cold, omit butter.

SAUERKRAUT

"To get the sweetest and most digestible sauerkraut, it should be made the day after full moon," says the Pennsylvania Dutch student of moon lore.

Select mature firm heads of cabbage, preferably white. Remove outer leaves and wash them. Weigh the cabbage in 5-pound lots and shred. For each 5 pounds use 3 tablespoons salt. Mix the salt thoroughly with the shredded cabbage.

Pack in layers in a clean stone crock, pressing down firmly with a wooden stumper or potato masher. Brine should rise as each layer is stumped down. When crock is nearly full, or all of cabbage is used, cover with washed outer leaves. Cover these with a piece of clean cloth and a plate. Weight it down with a big stone. Tie muslin over the crock and store in a cool place, 60° to 70°.

Every other day remove scum which forms. Each time remove the cloth, wipe the sides of the crock, and wash the plate. Replace, using a clean cloth. (Wash and boil the one removed to use the next time). In about three weeks the kraut is cured. Either cover with paraffin or pack in jars and process in boiling water for 30 minutes.

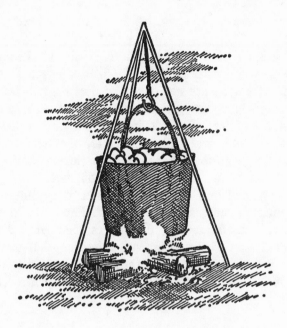

Sweets and Sours

GREAT publicity has been given to the Pennsylvania Dutch "Seven Sweets and Seven Sours." Actually, we don't bother to count them. There might be eight sours and only five sweets, or vice versa. At one time, some *Hausfrau* may have served precisely seven sweets and seven sours on her table, but most scholars today accept this as a myth. Pennsylvania Dutch people crave pickled fruits and vegetables to spice their hearty fare, and have them for almost every meal. One farmer even had pickles with his daily breakfast fare. When there are dinner guests, little dishes of various sweets and sours fill up the table until there is no more of the white tablecloth showing through.

What are the Sweets and Sours? When the Pennsylvania Dutch housewife speaks of them, she is usually referring to the fruits and vegetables she has preserved. For the non-Dutch who are interested in counting the Sweets and Sours in any given meal, the list of Sweets should include the jams, jellies, fruits, puddings, cookies, and desserts. As for the Sours, they are the meats and vegetables that have been pickled. Chow Chow* and Corn Relish* are the popular combinations of vegetables, and are most delicious. They are an asset to any meal course.

It is amazing that canning is still so important in an area where there are freezers in the homes, and fresh fruits are available all year. The total amount of canning has diminished, but there is still the craving for those home-canned Sweets and Sours. One bachelor cans 400 pints of Sours just for himself!

GRAPE BUTTER

(5 6-ounce glasses)

1 quart grapes (Blue Concord)
2 pounds sugar
3 tablespoons water

Wash, stem, and measure the grapes. Add the sugar and water and stir thoroughly. Boil 20 minutes. Strain and pour into glasses. Seal with paraffin.

PEAR BUTTER

(7 pints)

The amount of Pear Butter our grandmothers made was unbelievable. Almost every family had at least one pear tree in their yard in her generation. Now, there are fewer pear trees and much less pear butter.

5 pounds pears
2 pounds cooking apples
5 pounds sugar

Pare and core the pears and apples and cook separately. When soft, mash, mix together, and add sugar. Boil until thick.

APPLE BUTTER

(*Lottwaerrick*)

Adapted Oven Method

(5 quarts)

In the Pennsylvania Dutch dialect, apple butter is called *lottwaerrick*. The word is often linked with *schmierkase,** the Pennsylvania Dutch type of cottage cheese, and the two, according to some self-appointed authorities, should never be separated. It is true that rye bread is never any better than when it is spread with a thick layer of *lottwaerrick* and topped with *schmierkase*. It is a good combination for any kind of bread.

Apple butter-boiling was a custom brought here from the Palatinate where other kinds of fruit were cooked in the same manner—many hours over the open fire. It calls for a party, when bushels of apples are made into gallons of apple butter in a process that lasts all day or even several days. Many hands are required to pare the apples, cut the *schnitz* (apple slices), and, last but not least, to stir and stir and stir some more. In past generations, apple butter-boiling time was the social event of the season, when young couples gathered to take their turns in "schnitzing" and stirring. Although the apple butter is still boiled the same way, the younger generation seems no longer interested in "schnitzing parties!"

1 peck sweet cooking apples	*2 teaspoons cinnamon*
1 quart cider	*½ teaspoon cloves*
1 quart water	*½ teaspoon ground allspice*
10 cups sugar	

Wash apples, rubbing thoroughly if they have been sprayed. Core and cut into eighths. (Do not peel.) Add cider and water and cook until apples are soft. Press through strainer. Put into a large kettle that will fit in your oven. (I use 2 roasters.) Mix in 5 cups of the sugar.

Bake in 350° oven. Every half hour, stir with a wooden spoon. (A timer is an excellent reminder!) After an hour of cooking, add remaining sugar and spices. Cook 3 more hours or until the butter is thickened and dark red. Pour into sterilized jars and seal.

TOMATO PRESERVES

(12 6-ounce glasses)

5 pounds ripe tomatoes	*1 sliced lemon*
8 cups sugar	*1 sliced orange*

Peel and quarter the tomatoes. Peeling is quickly done by scalding in boiling water for 30 seconds and then plunging into cold water for another 30 seconds. To quartered tomatoes add the sugar and allow to stand overnight. Drain off syrup and boil until it is thick. Add tomatoes, sliced lemon, and orange. Cook over low heat until transparent. Pour into jelly glasses and cover with paraffin.

RHUBARB AND STRAWBERRY JAM

(8 6-ounce glasses)

4 cups slightly mashed strawberries
3 cups rhubarb, cut in ½-inch pieces
4½ cups sugar

Mix the ingredients and bring to a boil slowly, stirring until sugar is dissolved. Continue slow cooking until jam thickens. This will take about 35 minutes. Skim off the foam several times. Put into sterilized jars and seal with paraffin.

RHUBARB SAUCE

(Serves 6)

Perhaps a recipe without proportions will be the most practical here. Measure rhubarb that has been cut in ½-inch pieces and cook with half that much sugar, and water equal to one fourth the amount of sugar. If that is too much arithmetic for you, try this one:

4 cups rhubarb, washed and cut in ½-inch pieces
2 cups sugar
½ cup water

Cook rhubarb with sugar and water for 10 minutes or until rhubarb is soft.

RHUBARB AND STRAWBERRIES
(Serves 8)

Prepare Rhubarb Sauce,* adding 1 or 2 cups of strawberries
to cook with the rhubarb. Even though you use only 1 cup of
berries, the sauce will be delicious. Two cups will make it
scrumptious.

KIMMEL CHERRIES

A superb garnish for ham. Very easy to make.

Cover seeded sour cherries with vinegar and let stand 12
hours. Put into a colander and let drain for 2 hours.
Measure cherries and mix with them an equal part of sugar.
Cover and keep in a cool place for 9 days, stirring once a day.
(It takes this long to dissolve the sugar.) Without heating, pack
in jars and seal.

SPICED SECKEL PEARS
(5 pints)

7 pounds seckel pears	*1 tablespoon whole*
6 cups sugar	*cloves*
2 cups cider vinegar	*6 2-inch cinnamon*
1 cup water	*sticks*

Peel the whole pears, but do not core or take off stems.
Combine the sugar, vinegar, and water in a large kettle and
bring to a boil. Tie spices in a muslin bag and boil in syrup for
30 minutes. Add pears and cook until tender. With a spoon,
carefully place pears in sterilized jars. Place lids on jars but do

not tighten. Boil syrup rapidly for another 30 minutes. Pour over fruit and seal jars.

RHUBARB AND ORANGES

(Serves 8)

Prepare Rhubarb Sauce.*
When cool, add 2 oranges, peeled and sliced.

LEMON BUTTER

(2 cups)

A delicious spread for crackers. It keeps very well under refrigeration.

5 eggs, well beaten
2 cups sugar

grated rind and juice of
2 lemons
3 tablespoons butter

Thoroughly blend the eggs and sugar. Add the juice and rind of the lemons and the butter. Cook in the top of a double boiler over hot water, keeping water just under the boiling point. Stir while it thickens. Cool. Cover and refrigerate.

SPICED PEACHES

(6 pints)

6 pounds peaches
6 cups sugar
3 tablespoons whole
  cloves

1 3-inch stick cinnamon
1 pint vinegar

Peel, halve, and pit the peaches. Combine sugar, spices, and vinegar and bring to a boil. Drop in the peaches and cook only until tender to the touch of a fork. Pack in sterilized jars and fill with the syrup.

PICKLED CANTALOUPE

(4 pints)

3 pounds cantaloupe
squares
1½ cups sugar

½ cup vinegar
2 cups water

Pare the cantaloupe, remove the seeds, and cut into 1×2-inch pieces. Combine the sugar and vinegar with water and heat. When sugar is dissolved, add cantaloupe and simmer until fruit is clear, about 45 minutes. Pack into jars and seal.

Note: If desired, 1 tablespoon of pickling spices, tied in a spice bag, can be cooked with the melon for the last 15 minutes.

PICKLED WATERMELON

(4 pints)

Prepare rind by cutting into inch strips. Slice away pink flesh, peel off the green rind, then cut strips neatly into diamonds, squares, or triangles. Proceed as in recipe for Pickled Cantaloupe.*

FOURTEEN-DAY SWEET PICKLES

(8 quarts)

Truly, the processing can be more fun than bother. You will need a 2-gallon crock and a plate to use as its cover. The original recipe began: "Cover the pickles with salt water that is strong enough to hold an egg." Don't worry! I measured it for you.

2 gallons pickles, 3- to 4-inch size	1 tablespoon whole allspice
2 cups salt	1 tablespoon celery seed
3 tablespoons alum	5 2-inch cinnamon sticks
2 tablespoons whole mixed pickling spice	2 quarts vinegar
	1 quart water
	8 cups sugar

First day: Wash pickles and place in a 2-gallon crock. Dissolve salt in 4 quarts water and pour over pickles. Cover. Stir once a day for 7 days.

Eighth day: Drain pickles and cover with fresh boiling water.

Ninth day: Drain again and cover with fresh boiling water to which the alum has been added.

Tenth day: Drain. Cover with hot vinegar syrup made thus: Make a spice bag by tying the spices in an 8-inch square of muslin. Combine the 2 quarts of vinegar with the quart of water and *just 2* cups sugar. Add the spice bag to this and bring to a boil. Pour over the pickles. Leave spice bag with pickles.

Eleventh day: Drain vinegar into kettle. Boil with spice bag and 2 additional cups sugar. Pour over pickles.

Twelfth day: Same as eleventh day, again adding 2 more cups sugar.

Thirteenth day: Same as twelfth day.

Fourteenth day: Pack pickles into jars. Fill with boiling syrup. Seal. Discard spice bag.

BREAD-AND-BUTTER PICKLES

(10 pints)

My favorite pickle recipe! In fact, it seems to be everybody's favorite.

½ cup salt
1 gallon cucumbers,
   sliced very thin
8 small white onions,
   sliced

2 green peppers, sliced
   in thin strips
1 quart crushed ice

Mix salt with the three vegetables. Bury the ice in the mixture, then cover and let stand 3 hours. Drain thoroughly.

MAKE A PICKLING SYRUP OF THE FOLLOWING:

5 cups sugar
½ teaspoon turmeric
½ teaspoon ground
   cloves
2 tablespoons mustard
   seed

1 teaspoon celery seed
3 cups vinegar
2 cups water

Combine above ingredients and heat to almost boiling. Add the cucumbers and bring to a boil. Pack in jars and seal.

CRISP PICKLE MIX

(8 pints)

Cucumbers, onions, and cauliflower are put together for this interesting pickle mix.

15 medium-size
   cucumbers
4 large onions
3 cups cauliflowerets
1 green pepper, cut in
   1-inch squares
3 cloves garlic
⅓ cup salt

2 trays ice cubes
5 cups sugar
2 tablespoons mustard
   seed
1½ teaspoons celery
   seed
1 teaspoon turmeric
3 cups cider vinegar

Combine vegetables and add garlic and salt. Cover with ice cubes and mix well. Let stand 3 hours. Drain well. Add remaining ingredients to vegetables and heat just to boiling. Seal in hot jars.

BEAN PICKLE (Two-day process)

(12 pints)

5 cucumbers
2 tablespoons salt
1 gallon string beans
1 quart celery, cut in
   ½-inch pieces (about 8
   stalks)
4 green peppers

2 tablespoons whole
   pickling spice
1 tablespoon celery seed
2 teaspoons turmeric
6 cups sugar
2 quarts vinegar
1 quart water

Wash cucumbers and slice them very thin. Add salt and enough cold water to cover. Mix well and let stand overnight. Next day, clean beans and break in half, or smaller if desired. Cook beans and celery separately until almost tender. Drain. Combine with drained cucumbers and remaining ingredients, putting spices in muslin bag. Cook for 10 minutes. Remove spice bag. Put into hot sterilized jars and seal.

SWEET PICKLE RINGS

(5 pints)

12 medium cucumbers	*2 cups vinegar*
1 tablespoon salt	*36 whole cloves*
2 cups sugar	*1 teaspoon turmeric*

Cut cucumbers into ⅛-inch slices. There should be enough to measure 3 quarts. Add salt and mix lightly. Let stand 2 hours, then press out liquid without bruising cucumbers. Add remaining ingredients and enough water to cover. Heat to boiling point and can.

PEPPER RELISH

(7 pints)

18 red peppers	*1 tablespoon salt*
18 green peppers	*1 quart vinegar*
6 onions	*3 cups sugar*

Put the peppers and onions through food chopper separately. Pour boiling water over the peppers and let stand 5 minutes. Drain. Repeat. Cover with boiling water the third time and let stand 15 minutes. Add the chopped onions, salt, vinegar, and sugar. Boil for 15 minutes. Pack into jars and seal.

PEPPER RELISH WITH CABBAGE

(5 pints)

8 green peppers	*2 tablespoons salt*
8 red peppers	*½ cup diced celery*
12 onions	*1 cup sugar*
1 medium head cabbage	*3 cups vinegar*

Put the peppers, onions, and cabbage through food chopper using coarse blade. It is not necessary to keep them separate. Cover with boiling water. Simmer 15 minutes, then drain. Add the remaining ingredients and boil for about 50 minutes or until relish thickens. Put into jars and seal.

CHOW CHOW I

(8 pints)

A delightful medley of vegetables that are cooked separately and then combined in a pickling mixture. 'Tis a relish that will enhance every dinner. Do try it. If you have your own vegetable garden, you might want to change the proportions of vegetables according to what you have on hand. If you do not have a garden, use the following recipe that has been adapted for twentieth-century city folk.

*1 pint each of the
following:
sliced cucumbers
chopped sweet peppers
chopped cabbage
sliced onions
chopped green
    tomatoes
Lima beans
cut green beans*

*sliced carrots
cut celery
2 tablespoons celery seed
4 tablespoons mustard
    seed
1 quart vinegar
2 cups water
4 cups sugar
4 tablespoons turmeric*

Soak cucumbers, peppers, cabbage, onions, and tomatoes in salt water overnight, using ½ cup salt to 2 quarts water. Drain in the morning. Cook Lima beans, green beans, carrots, and celery, each separately, until tender. Drain. Combine soaked and cooked vegetables with remaining ingredients. Cook 10 minutes. Put into sterilized jars and seal.

CHOW CHOW II

(Using 10-ounce packages of frozen vegetables)

(14 pints)

This is a modern recipe that utilizes frozen vegetables to make the "end-of-the-summer relish," as the Pennsylvania Dutch people often call it.

3 packages frozen Lima beans

2 packages frozen green beans

2 packages frozen yellow beans

3 packages frozen cauliflower

1 quart celery, cut in ½-inch pieces

1 quart carrot slices

4 cups sugar

2 tablespoons salt

2 tablespoons celery seed

2 tablespoons mustard seed

1 tablespoon turmeric

5 cups vinegar

5 cups water

1 15-ounce jar sweet pickle slices

2 8-ounce jars sweet gherkins

2 6-ounce jars cocktail onions

Open packages of frozen vegetables to thaw. Cook celery and carrots 30 minutes. While these are cooking, put sugar, salt, celery seed, mustard seed, turmeric, vinegar, and water in an 8-quart kettle. Bring to a boil. Add frozen vegetables that have been partly thawed to the vinegar mixture. Boil 5 minutes.

When celery and carrots are tender, drain first, then add to hot vegetables. Also add the pickles and onions. Bring to a boil and boil for 5 minutes again. Seal at once in jars.

CORN RELISH

(10 pints)

20 *ears of corn*	2 *tablespoons dry*
6 *green peppers*	*mustard*
6 *red peppers*	2 *tablespoons celery seed*
4 *large onions*	2 *tablespoons salt*
1 *large head cabbage*	1 *tablespoon turmeric*
4 *cups sugar*	5 *cups vinegar*
	1 *cup water*

Cut corn off cobs. Chop the peppers, onions, and cabbage. Add all of remaining ingredients to the corn and chopped vegetables. Cook together for 20 minutes, then put into sterilized jars and seal.

GREEN TOMATO AND CABBAGE RELISH

(8 pints)

4 *cups chopped onions*	6 *cups sugar*
4 *cups chopped cabbage*	1 *tablespoon celery seed*
4 *cups chopped green*	2 *tablespoons mustard*
tomatoes (about 10)	*seed*
12 *green peppers*	2 *teaspoons turmeric*
6 *red peppers*	4 *cups cider vinegar*
½ *cup salt*	2 *cups water*

Put vegetables through food chopper, using coarse blade. Cover with ½ cup salt and let stand overnight. Rinse well and drain. Put vegetable mixture into a kettle, then add remaining ingredients. Heat to boiling, then simmer 3 minutes. Seal in sterilized jars.

MUSTARD BEANS I

(12 pints)

To be served hot or cold as a relish.

1 peck string beans (preferably yellow)	4 cups sugar
6 quarts water	3 cups vinegar
5 teaspoons salt	6 cups water
1 cup (9-ounce jar) prepared mustard	

Cut ends from beans and break in half. Cook in salted water for 30 minutes or until tender. Combine remaining ingredients and heat to boiling. When beans are tender, drain. Pour boiling mustard liquid over hot beans. Fill jars and seal.

MUSTARD BEANS II

(1 pint)

Quick and easy method with canned beans.

1 cup sugar	¼ teaspoon salt
½ cup cider vinegar	1-pound can wax beans, drained
3 tablespoons prepared mustard	

Combine all ingredients except the beans; bring to a boil, stirring until sugar is dissolved. Add beans and simmer for 5 minutes. Cool, then cover and refrigerate overnight. It will keep indefinitely. Serve as a relish.

SUMMER MINCEMEAT

(1 gallon)

A pie filling made from green tomatoes. Prepare it in the summer or fall for winter enjoyment.

8 large green tomatoes	*½ cup butter*
8 large tart apples	*1 teaspoon salt*
1 cup vinegar	*1 pound seedless raisins*
1 cup molasses	*1 teaspoon cinnamon*
3 cups brown sugar	*½ teaspoon ginger*

Core the tomatoes and apples but do not peel. Put both through food chopper and combine with remaining ingredients. Pour into a large kettle and mix thoroughly. Bring to a boil and keep boiling for 5 minutes. Immediately put into jars and seal. Each quart will make a delicious mince pie—mock mince pie, of course.

PICKLED RED BEETS

(1 pint)

In Pennsylvania Dutch country the word "beets" is never used alone. One always says "red beets."

1 number 2 can beets	*1 teaspoon salt*
1 cup vinegar	*4 cloves*
½ cup sugar	*2-inch stick cinnamon*

Drain and measure juice from beets. Add enough water to make 1 cup. To this juice add the vinegar, sugar, salt, and spices, then bring to a boil. Pour hot liquid over beets. Let stand 24 hours.

RED BEET EGGS

(Pickled Eggs)

(½ dozen)

Enjoyed for their flavor throughout the year, but a must for every picnic. The color they give to the picnic table is just a bonus feature.

Prepare Pickled Red Beets.* After beets have been pickled, remove them and replace with hard-cooked eggs. Let stand in juice 8 to 12 hours so that flavor penetrates whole egg.

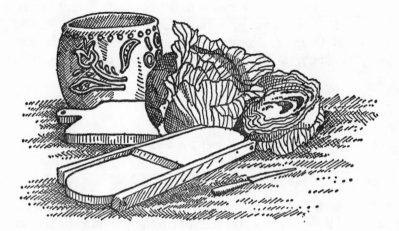

Salads and Salad Dressings

IF you picked up this Pennsylvania Dutch cookbook to find an unusual salad for the Bridge Club Salad Luncheon, you have the wrong book. Traditional Pennsylvania Dutch salads are not that kind. They are very simple vegetable salads, used as an accompaniment to the meat course.

Most of the salad dressings are cooked dressings, and are the important part of the salads. Until recently, each cook made her own. Now, commercial firms have begun to sell them—even the popular boiled Bacon Dressing.* It can be bought ready to heat and serve.

Bacon dressings vary. They may be made with either a water, milk, or cream base. All of them are cooked dressings and served hot. Bacon dressing on young dandelion leaves, spring garden leaf lettuce, or late-summer endive is the Pennsylvania Dutchman's first choice in salads. As a close second, he rates cabbage slaw. In this category, Pepper Cabbage* is the top favorite. Fruit salads were nonexistent until recent years. Canned fruits are now occasionally served on lettuce without any effort to present a thing of beauty. In this "plain and fancy" country, salads have never reached the fancy stage.

MOTHER'S POTATO SALAD

(Serves 8)

Ever since this recipe appeared in my first cookbook, people have repeatedly told me how much they enjoyed using it. Mother always made this salad for picnics as well as for Sunday night suppers throughout the summer. It is very important that it be prepared ahead to allow 8 hours for the potatoes to absorb the flavor of the dressing.

4 large potatoes	1 tablespoon flour
1 onion, minced	½ cup water
5 stems of celery, cut fine	½ cup vinegar
2 hard-cooked eggs, chopped	2 tablespoons butter
1 egg, beaten	½ teaspoon salt
½ cup sugar	⅛ teaspoon pepper
	1 tablespoon prepared mustard (optional)

Wash the potatoes and boil in salted water until soft. Peel. Slice into a large bowl in alternate layers with the onion, celery, and hard-cooked eggs. Make the salad dressing by combining the remaining ingredients in the order given and stirring after each addition. Bring to a boil, stirring constantly, and simmer a few minutes longer until dressing thickens. Cool slightly. Mix lightly with potatoes. Cover and refrigerate for 8 hours or longer.

TOMATO SALAD

(Serves 4)

3 large tomatoes
salt and pepper to taste
1 tablespoon sugar

1 to 2 teaspoons minced
  onion
¼ cup vinegar
¼ cup water

Scald tomatoes, then peel. Cut thick slices into a vegetable serving dish. Season with salt, pepper, sugar, and onion. Dilute vinegar with water and pour over tomatoes.

CARROT SALAD

(Serves 6)

Can be served with or without lettuce.

2 cups grated carrots
1 cup shredded cabbage
½ onion, chopped fine
1 egg
½ cup sugar
1 tablespoon flour
½ cup vinegar

½ cup water
2 tablespoons butter
½ teaspoon salt
dash of pepper
1 tablespoon prepared
  mustard

Toss together the grated carrots, cabbage, and onion. In a small bowl beat the egg, then add to it the combined sugar and flour, beating until smooth. Slowly add vinegar, water, and remaining ingredients, mixing well.

Cook dressing over medium heat until thick, stirring all the while. Set pan in a bowl of cold water for 5 minutes to cool. Add to vegetables. Serve.

LETTUCE AND EGG SALAD

(Serves 4)

A simple salad that can be tossed together in a matter of minutes. A splendid way to serve the garden leaf lettuce grown in most Pennsylvania gardens.

3 cups early leaf lettuce,
* or ½ head lettuce*
2 hard-cooked eggs,
* sliced*

¼ cup cream
2 tablespoons sugar
1 tablespoon vinegar
½ teaspoon salt

Coarsely cut up the lettuce and cover with sliced eggs. Combine the cream, sugar, vinegar, and salt. Pour over lettuce and egg. Toss lightly and serve.

LETTUCE AND ONION SALAD

(Serves 6)

½ head lettuce
½ cup chopped onion
½ cup water
2 tablespoons vinegar

2 tablespoons sugar
½ teaspoon salt
2 hard-cooked eggs

Break up lettuce coarsely and mix it with the chopped onion. Measure ½ cup water in a measuring cup. Add to it the vinegar, sugar, and salt. Stir to mix and dissolve sugar.

Divide the lettuce and onion into 4 or 5 fruit saucers, then slice hard-cooked eggs on top of lettuce. Cover with vinegar dressing and serve.

APPLE AND CABBAGE COLESLAW

(Serves 6)

2 cups shredded cabbage
1 cup diced apples
½ cup raisins (optional)

¼ teaspoon salt
⅓ cup Cooked Salad
   Dressing*

Toss all ingredients together lightly.

PEPPER CABBAGE

(Serves 6 to 8)

A very special coleslaw! This one is served each year at the Pennsylvania Folk Festival in Kutztown, Pennsylvania. Hundreds of visitors there have requested the recipe.

4 cups shredded cabbage
½ green pepper, chopped
   fine
1 stem celery, cut fine
¼ cup grated carrot
   (optional)

1 teaspoon salt
5 tablespoons sugar
½ cup water
5 tablespoons vinegar

Combine all ingredients, mixing well. If refrigerated, will keep well for several days.

TURNIP SLAW

(Serves 6 to 8)

Prepare exactly as Cream Slaw* but substitute 4 cups coarsely grated turnips for the cabbage. Water can be substituted for the cream.

CREAM SLAW

(Serves 6 to 8)

4 cups shredded cabbage   *5 tablespoons vinegar*
1 teaspoon salt   *2 tablespoons minced*
3 tablespoons sugar   *chives or green onion*
½ cup cream   *tops (optional)*

Shred cabbage with grater or cut on slaw cutter. Sprinkle with salt and sugar, then pound well with a potato masher. Pour cream over it and mix thoroughly. Add vinegar and chives and mix again.

COOKED DRESSING FOR COLESLAW

(1 pint)

2 eggs, beaten   *½ cup vinegar*
1 cup sugar   *1 tablespoon butter*
½ teaspoon salt   *½ cup cream*

In the top of a double boiler combine all ingredients but the cream. Cook until thick. Cool; then add the cream.

SOUR CREAM SALAD DRESSING

(1 pint)

Especially good for coleslaw or sliced cucumbers.

1 pint sour cream   *2 tablespoons diced*
2 tablespoons chopped   *celery (optional)*
chives   *2 tablespoons sugar*
½ cup minced onion   *2 tablespoons vinegar*

Mix ingredients in the order given. Combine with shredded cabbage or sliced cucumbers. Chill for a half hour before serving.

COOKED SALAD DRESSING

(1 cup)

4 *tablespoons sugar*	2 *whole eggs or yolks of*
4 *tablespoons vinegar*	3, *beaten*
2 *tablespoons water*	3 *tablespoons butter*

Combine all ingredients in a small saucepan. Bring to a boil and cook over medium heat until thickened, about 2 minutes.

BACON DRESSING I

(2 cups)

This is the hot dressing that is poured over dandelion. With the first sign of spring, comes the craving for a mess of dandelion. Out in the fields and pastures you can see grandmothers and children with little baskets and knives looking for young dandelion greens. Many have come to think of dandelion as a spring health tonic, just as necessary as sulphur and molasses.

4 *slices bacon, cut in*	3 *tablespoons flour*
inch pieces	½ *teaspoon salt*
1½ *cups water*	2 *tablespoons sugar*
1 *beaten egg*	*pinch dry mustard*
2 *tablespoons vinegar*	*(optional)*

Fry bacon until crisp; then remove from fat. Remove pan from heat. Mix other ingredients in a gravy shaker, shaking vigorously, then pour into pan with bacon fat. Return pan to medium heat and bring to a boil, stirring constantly.

Add half of bacon to hot dressing and save rest of bacon to garnish top of salad. Pour hot dressing over dandelion greens, endive, or lettuce. Serve immediately.

BACON DRESSING II

(1½ cups. Serves 6)

Mixing in a shaker insures a smooth dressing.

4 slices bacon, cut in
  inch pieces
½ cup sugar
½ teaspoon salt

1 tablespoon cornstarch
1 beaten egg
¼ cup vinegar
1 cup cream

Fry bacon pieces slowly until brown, then drain on paper towels. Remove pan from heat while you mix other ingredients in a gravy shaker or pint jar, shaking vigorously. From shaker pour dressing into pan with fat and bring to a boil slowly, stirring constantly. Cook to desired thickness, then pour over cut dandelion greens, endive, or lettuce. Top with bacon. Serve immediately.

CREAMED CUCUMBERS

(Serves 4 to 6)

Allow enough time to refrigerate salted cucumber slices several hours.

2 cucumbers
1 teaspoon salt
½ cup cream

1 tablespoon vinegar
1 tablespoon sugar

Pare cucumbers and slice very thin. Add salt, then refrigerate for several hours. Rinse with cold water, squeezing out the salt. Make the dressing by combining the cream, vinegar, and sugar. Pour over cucumber slices and serve.

Fritters, Fillings, Potpie, Et Cetera

THE odds and ends of this regional cookery are indeed fascinating and distinctive. There are numerous recipes that just will not fit anywhere else, and are placed in this chapter—such items as Funnel Cakes,* Hex Waffles,* Stewed Crackers,* and Huddlestrow.*

There is a tremendous amount of deep-fat frying in Pennsylvania Dutch cookery. In the chapter on Breadstuffs, recipes are given for the various doughnuts and fasnachts fried in this way. This chapter has the fritters, Funnel Cakes,* Snavely Sticks,* and Hex Waffles* that are deep-fat-fried and served for midmorning lunches and suppers. In the Potato chapter there are Potato Balls* that are also deep-fat-fried.

There are also deep-fat-fried foods not included in the book, since jet age cooks aren't likely to make them. Dandelion flowers and elderberry blossoms are two that have been omitted.

Do you feel adventurous? Pick the blossoms without stems and promptly dip in a fritter batter to deep-fat-fry them.

A section of the chapter is devoted to boiled Potpie* recipes. Boiled potpie is a traditional dinner feature frequently served in Pennsylvania Dutch families. Although the stew is basically the same, there are small differences in the way the cooks prepare the dough. Four potpie recipes are given. If you are of Pennsylvania Dutch descent, you can try the recipe your grandmother used. If you have never tasted boiled potpie, try all four, then decide which you like the best.

KASHA KUCHA

(*Cherry Cakes*)

(20 2-inch balls)

Here is Hoffmans' own recipe for the popular Kasha Kucha they make at the annual Kutztown Pennsylvania Folk Festival. Cherry cakes are delicious served hot or cold.

2 eggs	4 cups flour
1 cup sugar	2 cups sweet or sour
1 teaspoon butter	cherries, drained
½ teaspoon salt	shortening for deep-fat
½ teaspoon baking soda	fryer
3 teaspoons baking	powdered sugar
powder	(optional)
1 cup milk	

Beat the eggs and add to them the sugar and butter. Cream together. Mix together the salt, baking soda, and baking powder, and add to creamed mixture. To this add the milk and flour alternately. Fold in the cherries. Drop from a tablespoon into deep fat that is heated to 365°. Shaking powdered sugar over them when serving makes them doubly attractive.

APPLE FRITTERS

(Serves 6)

1 cup flour
1½ teaspoons baking
  powder
1¼ teaspoons salt
2 tablespoons sugar

⅔ cup milk
1 egg, beaten
4 large cooking apples
table syrup

Sift together the first 4 ingredients. Slowly add combined milk and beaten egg. Beat until smooth.

Pare and core apples, leaving them whole. Slice each apple crosswise into 4 slices. Dip each slice into batter and then into hot shortening ¼ inch deep in skillet. Fry until brown, turning once to brown on other side. Drain on paper towels. Serve with table syrup.

CHERRY FRITTERS

(Serves 6)

A treat for breakfast or supper.

1 cup sifted flour
1 teaspoon baking
  powder
2 tablespoons sugar
½ teaspoon salt
1 egg

⅔ cup milk
2 cups drained, pitted
  sour cherries
3 tablespoons shortening
molasses or table syrup

Sift together the flour, baking powder, sugar, and salt. Beat the egg, then add milk to it. Combine the liquid with the flour mixture gradually. Beat until smooth. Add cherries and mix well.

Drop from a large spoon into a skillet that has melted shortening in it. When cakes are full of bubbles, turn to brown on other side. Serve with molasses or table syrup.

TOMATO FRITTERS

(Serves 6)

2 cups canned tomatoes (1 number 2 can)	1 teaspoon baking powder
½ teaspoon salt	1 cup flour
1 teaspoon sugar	vegetable shortening
1 egg	syrup

With a kitchen shears, cut through tomatoes until there are no big pieces left. To the tomatoes add the salt and sugar.

In another bowl, beat the egg, then add to it the baking powder and flour. Mix well. Drop from tablespoon into ¼ inch hot shortening in skillet. Fry until golden brown. Serve with table syrup.

CORN FRITTERS

(Serves 6)

What can be better than Corn Fritters made with fresh corn? Using canned corn in winter is next best. With either, we serve molasses or syrup. That good old molasses barrel in the country store will soon be a thing of the past, I fear. In the Pennsylvania Dutch area we still have barrel molasses.

2 eggs
2 cups fresh grated
   corn or 1 can
   cream-style corn
2 tablespoons sugar
dash of black pepper

4 tablespoons flour
½ teaspoon baking
   powder
3 tablespoons milk
vegetable shortening
syrup or molasses

Beat the eggs. Add the corn to them. In a cup, mix together the sugar, pepper, flour, and baking powder. Add this mixture and milk to corn and eggs. Fry in ¼ inch hot shortening in frying pan. Brown on both sides. Serve at once with syrup.

FUNNEL CAKES

(Serves 6)

An interesting name for a snack item! At the annual Pennsylvania Folk Festival at Kutztown, Pennsylvania, Funnel Cakes are the most popular food item. Here, people are intrigued as they watch the fascinating process of frying Funnel Cakes. A waffle-like batter runs through a funnel into the hot fat in a swirling motion that forms rings around rings. In past years it was a wonderful item for the nine o'clock lunch of the harvesting farmer. Today it is ideal for coffee breaks.

2 eggs
1⅓ cups milk
2⅔ cups flour
4 tablespoons sugar
½ teaspoon salt

1 teaspoon baking
   powder
2 teaspoons baking soda
shortening
powdered sugar or syrup

Beat the eggs and add the milk to them. Sift the flour, sugar, salt, baking powder, and soda together. To these add the egg and milk. Beat until smooth.

Holding a finger over the bottom of the funnel, pour some batter into the funnel. Drop batter into hot deep fat, 375°, swirling it into circles from the center outward. Make each cake about 6 inches in diameter. Fry until golden brown, turning once. Serve warm with powdered sugar or syrup.

Note: Funnel should have ⅝-inch opening.

HEX WAFFLES

(20 Rosette Wafers)

Hex Waffle irons are now a collector's item. Find them, if you can!

1 egg	*⅛ teaspoon vanilla*
1 teaspoon sugar	*shortening for deep-fat*
⅛ teaspoon salt	*fryer*
½ cup milk	*powdered sugar*
½ cup flour	

In a small bowl beat the egg. Add to it the sugar, salt, milk, flour, and vanilla, and beat until blended. Let set for 1 hour or more. Heat the wafer iron in the shortening until it is very hot (370°). Wipe off the excess fat with a handful of paper towels.

Dip the hot iron into the batter to about ¾ of its depth, then submerge completely in the hot fat for about 30 seconds. Lift off the Hex Waffle with a cloth. Before making next Hex Waffle, dip iron in fat again and then wipe off excess fat as before. Repeat before frying each Hex Waffle.

Serve immediately after sprinkling powdered sugar on them. Do not attempt to keep them more than 8 hours, as they lose their crispness quickly.

POTPIE CRACKERS

(Serves 6 to 8)

Steamed in hot chicken gravy, they are "wonderful good." Tiny baked squares of pastry enriched with butter and moistened with milk—these are Potpie Crackers.

⅓ cup lard	1 teaspoon salt
⅓ cup butter	½ cup milk
2½ cups sifted flour	2 cups chicken gravy

Cut the lard and butter into the flour and salt until it is the size of peas. Add the milk very gradually, stirring lightly until all the flour is dampened.

Taking ⅓ of the dough at a time, roll out on a floured board to ⅛-inch thickness. Carefully lift around rolling pin and transfer to cookie sheet. Cut into 1-inch squares with a knife or pastry wheel. Bake for 12 minutes at 400°.

To serve: Put the crackers into a tureen or casserole and cover with the hot gravy. Steam for 5 minutes, stirring once. Serve.

SNAVELY STICKS

(*Recipe used by several generations of the Snavely family*)

(Serves 6 to 8)

Another deep-fat-fried finger food. This one is also known as Plowlines or *Streivlin*. Some cooks like to add a bit of sugar to the dough or sprinkle the sticks with powdered sugar after frying. Sweetened or not, they are an excellent accompaniment to today's salads and soups.

2 *eggs*   2 *teaspoons salt*
1 *cup coffee cream*   4 *cups sifted flour*

Beat the eggs and add to the cream. Add the salt and flour gradually to form a stiff dough. Roll out the dough, a quarter at a time, to a very thin sheet. Cut this round of dough into sections 4 or 5 inches wide. Cut each section (using a pastry wheel, if you have one) into half-inch strips, cutting only to within 1 inch of outer edge so that section stays intact.

Fry 1 or 2 sections at a time, depending on size of deep-fat fryer. Fat should be heated to 365°. Turning once, fry until sticks have turned a light brown. Serve warm.

OYSTER FILLING

(Serves 6 to 8)

8 *slices day-old bread*   1 *small onion, minced*
2 *eggs*   ¼ *cup celery, cut fine*
1 *cup milk*   2 *tablespoons butter*
1 *teaspoon salt and dash*   1 *pint stewing oysters*
  of pepper
2 *tablespoons chopped*
  parsley or 1 teaspoon
  dried parsley

Cube bread. Beat eggs and combine with milk and seasonings. Pour this over bread cubes. Lightly brown onion and celery in butter. Add to bread mixture, folding in lightly.

In a buttered casserole arrange alternate layers of the filling and oysters, using filling on the top and bottom layers. Bake for 1 hour in a medium oven (350°).

BREAD FILLING

(Enough for 5-pound fowl)

The eggs and milk make Pennsylvania Dutch dressing different. We like it so well that we sometimes serve it without the fowl. It is often baked in a casserole or fried in a skillet. An excellent substitute for potatoes.

1 egg, beaten
1 cup milk
6 cups soft breadcrumbs
1 small onion, minced
¼ cup celery, cut fine
2 tablespoons butter

1 teaspoon salt
⅛ teaspoon pepper
¼ teaspoon saffron
(optional)
2 tablespoons minced
parsley

Add beaten egg and milk to breadcrumbs. Sauté onions and celery in melted butter until brown. Add these and remaining seasonings to the breadcrumbs. Mix well.

Stuff fowl, or put into greased casserole and bake for 1 hour at 350°, or fry in a skillet over low heat.

POTPIE I

(Serves 8)

Every Pennsylvania Dutchman eats Potpie. Boiled with meat and potatoes, these squares of dough are really delicious.

2 cups flour
½ teaspoon salt
1 teaspoon baking
powder

2 tablespoons lard
1 egg, beaten
⅓ cup water

Combine dry ingredients. Cut the lard into the flour mixture until the pieces are very fine. Lightly stir in the beaten egg and water. Roll out very thin on floured board. Cut into 2-inch squares with knife or pastry wheel. Drop into boiling broth with meat and potatoes. Cook 20 minutes.

POTPIE II

(Serves 8)

This Potpie is called "the slippy kind," in contrast to Potpie I which has baking powder in it to make it light. Some like their potpie light and others like it slippy! Either one is good enough for me.

> *3 tablespoons shortening*   *1 egg*
> *2 cups flour, unsifted*   *milk (¼ to ½ cup)*
> *1 teaspoon salt*

Cut shortening into the flour and salt. Beat egg and add to it the dry ingredients and enough milk to make a soft dough. Roll half of dough very thin. Cut in 2-inch squares. Drop into boiling broth with meat and potatoes. Cook, covered, for 20 minutes.

POTPIE III

(Serves 8)

And some prefer this one! Have your pick!

> *3 cups sifted flour*   *1 cup water*
> *1 teaspoon salt*   *black pepper*
> *¼ cup shortening*

Mix together the flour, salt, shortening, and water as for pastry. Roll on floured board till ⅛ inch thick. Cut into 2-inch squares and drop into boiling broth. Add a copious amount of black pepper. Cover and cook for 30 minutes.

POTPIE IV

(Serves 6)

This one is more like noodle dough.

2 eggs, slightly beaten	*3 tablespoons milk*
¼ teaspoon salt	*2½ cups sifted flour*

Combine eggs, salt, and milk. Add flour and work in with your fingers. Dough should be dry, not sticky. When all flour is mixed in, roll dough (half at a time) on lightly floured board until very thin. Cut in 2-inch squares and drop into boiling broth. Cook for 20 minutes without removing lid of kettle.

STEWED CRACKERS

(Serves 4)

In Germany this dish is served today just as it was when our ancestors lived there. Today we substitute saltines for the S. S. Butter Crackers which we used to call Sunday School crackers and are no longer available. Stewed Crackers are not only served for breakfast and supper, but on "sick trays," as most Pennsylvania Dutchmen have experienced.

¼ pound saltines	*½ teaspoon salt*
1 cup boiling water	*dash of pepper*
2 tablespoons butter	*½ cup milk*

Put crackers into a tureen or covered casserole. Pour 1 cup boiling water over them. Cover tightly to steam for 5 minutes. Brown the butter and season with salt and pepper. Add milk to browned butter. When the milk is hot and the crackers have steamed 5 minutes, pour the butter and milk over them, give crackers an upside down turn, and cover for another 5 minutes.

FRIED CRACKERS

(Serves 4)

Stewed Crackers*　　　　*salt and pepper*
2 tablespoons butter　　　*jelly (optional)*
2 eggs

Prepare Stewed Crackers. Turn into a skillet that has the butter melted in it. Beat the eggs just slightly with a fork, then pour over the crackers. Season lightly and turn. When eggs are cooked, serve with jelly on top of crackers.

LIVER KNEPP

(*Liver Dumplings*)

(Serves 6 to 8)

3 slices bread　　　　　　*½ teaspoon salt*
½ pound liver　　　　　　*dash pepper*
1 small onion　　　　　　　*1 egg, beaten*
⅛ teaspoon cloves　　　　*1 cup flour*
⅛ teaspoon allspice　　　*beef broth, about 2*
½ teaspoon cinnamon　　　　*quarts*
½ teaspoon dried parsley

Break up bread in a medium-size bowl and cover with water. Grind raw liver and onion in food chopper. Squeeze water out of bread, then combine liver with bread. Add spices and seasonings. Stir in beaten egg and flour.

Drop from a tablespoon into boiling beef broth. Cook, covered, for 25 minutes.

CORN MEAL MUSH

(Serves 6)

Pennsylvania Corn Meal is roasted yellow corn meal that is the best corn meal found anywhere. Yes, I'm prejudiced.

1 tablespoon salt	*2 cups cold water*
2 cups corn meal	*4 cups boiling water*

Add salt to the corn meal and mix thoroughly with cold water. Place boiling water in upper part of double boiler. Slowly add the meal mixture to it, stirring constantly. Cover and cook for 2 hours, stirring 3 or 4 times.

Serve hot in soup dishes with milk and sugar poured over it. A spoonful of bran cereal sprinkled over the top is a flavorful addition.

FRIED MUSH

(Serves 6)

The Pennsylvania Dutch frequently enjoy Fried Mush served with "Puddin' Meat" that is made by their butchers. Fried Mush is a favorite combination.

Pour hot Corn Meal Mush* into loaf pan. When cold, cut into slices ½ inch thick. Dip each slice into flour and fry in hot corn oil slowly until outside is crisp and brown. Serve with molasses.

CORN PONE

(Serves 6)

Another supper dish that is eaten with milk.

2 eggs, well beaten	1 teaspoon baking soda
½ cup sugar	1 cup corn meal
½ teaspoon salt	1 cup flour
½ cup lard	sweetened milk
1 cup buttermilk	

Combine ingredients in the order given, mixing thoroughly after each addition. Turn into greased 8-inch square pan. Bake 30 minutes in a 350° oven. Serve square cuts in soup dishes with sweetened milk poured over it.

HUDDLESTROW

(Serves 4)

This is also called "Stirabout," and is surely a "mixed-up affair" which is the translation of Huddlestrow. It is actually a stiff pancake dough that is fried as a huge cake but then is chopped while it is browning. It is eaten for breakfast with syrup.

3 eggs	2 cups flour
1 cup water	2 tablespoons lard
½ teaspoon salt	syrup

Beat the eggs. Add the water, salt, and flour, beating until the dough is smooth. Turn it into a hot skillet in which the lard is melted. When the bottom has browned a bit, start chopping and turning with 2 knives until all is chopped in small pieces. Serve with syrup.

BOOCH-WAITZA GRIBBLE

(*Buckwheat Pieces*)

(Serves 4)

A very old way to serve buckwheat for supper.

1 cup buckwheat flour
½ teaspoon salt
¾ cup milk
1 tablespoon lard

2 tablespoons vegetable
  shortening
milk

Mix together the buckwheat flour, salt, and milk. Beat until smooth.

Melt lard and vegetable shortening in skillet. Drop buckwheat mixture into skillet from tablespoon. With pancake turner keep stirring and turning the mixture as it browns. Break up into small pieces while you stir. After about 5 minutes, when all is browned, remove from pan to soup plates. Serve with cold milk to pour over it.

BUCKWHEAT CAKES

(16 4-inch pancakes)

A traditional pancake that is made with yeast. In the days of the wood-burning kitchen stove, a crock of yeast-buckwheat mixture was kept on the back part of the stove from day to day. With this adapted recipe, part of the batter is mixed and set to rise overnight in the refrigerator.

½ package dry yeast (1 teaspoon)
¼ cup lukewarm water
1 cup cold water
1 cup buckwheat flour
½ cup all-purpose flour
¾ teaspoon salt

1 tablespoon table molasses
2 tablespoons melted butter
½ teaspoon soda, dissolved in ¼ cup hot water

Dissolve the yeast in lukewarm water, then add cold water. Into a 2-quart mixing bowl sift together the buckwheat flour, all-purpose flour, and salt. Stir in the yeast mixture and beat until smooth. Cover and place in refrigerator overnight.

In the morning add remaining ingredients and let stand at room temperature for 30 minutes. Bake on a hot greased griddle. Brown on both sides.

Note: Pork sausages are an excellent accompaniment for buckwheat cakes.

FLANNEL CAKES

(Serves 6)

An old-fashioned name for pancakes.

2 cups flour
1 teaspoon salt
3 teaspoons baking powder

2 cups milk
1 egg, beaten
1 tablespoon melted shortening

Mix and sift the flour, salt, and baking powder. Add the milk, beaten egg, and the shortening. Mix well. Drop by tablespoons on a hot griddle. When cakes are full of bubbles, turn to brown on other side.

CORN MEAL GRIDDLE CAKES

(Serves 6)

½ cup flour
2 cups corn meal
1 teaspoon salt
1 teaspoon baking powder

1 teaspoon baking soda
1 egg
2 cups buttermilk
2 tablespoons butter, melted

Put first 5 ingredients into the sifter and set aside momentarily. In a mixing bowl beat the egg and add the buttermilk to it. Sift into this egg and milk the dry ingredients. Stir quickly until all ingredients are blended. Stir in melted butter.

Bake on a griddle, turning once to brown other side. Turn when cakes are full of bubbles and outside edges are dry.

EGG BREAD

(Serves 4)

A very simple breakfast dish!

4 cups soft bread cubes
2 tablespoons butter
2 eggs, lightly beaten

1 cup milk
salt and pepper to taste

Brown the bread cubes in butter. Lift bread cubes from skillet and turn eggs into skillet. Pour in milk and seasonings. Just as eggs are beginning to set, add bread and mix thoroughly. Cook a few minutes longer until eggs are set and milk is absorbed.

NOODLES I

Homemade noodles are regularly served on the Pennsylvania Dutch dinner table. *Gschmelzte Nudle* is the dialect name for noodles that are drenched in browned butter with breadcrumbs.

2 eggs	1¾ cups flour, unsifted
1 tablespoon cold water	¼ teaspoon salt

Beat the eggs and add the water. Stir in the flour and salt. It will be necessary to knead with fingers to get it thoroughly mixed.

On a floured board roll out half of the dough at a time until paper-thin. Place sections on top of each other and roll up tightly like a jelly roll. Slice across the roll with a very sharp knife, making the noodles as thin as desired. Unroll and spread out to dry before storing.

NOODLES II

2 eggs	¼ teaspoon salt
2 tablespoons cream	1 cup flour
¼ teaspoon baking	
powder	

Beat the eggs and add the cream. Mix together the baking powder, salt, and flour, and add it to the eggs and cream. After stirring, it will be necessary to knead with fingers until the dough is thoroughly blended.

Taking half of the dough at a time, roll out on floured board until paper-thin. Place each round of dough on a cloth to partially dry. When edges appear dry, place one round on top of the other, then roll tightly as a jelly roll. Slice in very thin slices.

To store for future use, separate noodles and dry *thoroughly* before storing in covered container.

GSCHMELZTE NUDLE

(*Buttered Noodles*)

(Serves 6)

2 cups noodles	*3 tablespoons butter*
1½ quarts water	*¼ cup breadcrumbs*
1 teaspoon salt	

Drop 2 cups noodles into 1½ quarts boiling water. Add salt and boil for 20 minutes. Meanwhile make crumbs by melting and browning the three tablespoons of butter, then mixing in the breadcrumbs.

When noodles are cooked, drain and rinse with cold water. Put into serving dish and cover with prepared crumbs.

Desserts

IN the Pennsylvania Dutch household desserts are served with every meal: pie, cake, or cookies for breakfast; several desserts for dinner; one or more for supper. For dinner the assembly might include peaches, cherries in gelatin, cracker pudding (two or three puddings for company meals), cookies, and then apple pie "to top off on!"

The Pennsylvania Dutch can make a meal out of desserts. Some supper menus seem to be a sequence of desserts, or the main dish is a dessert. To us, Apple Dumplings* need not be a dessert. We have seconds and thirds! The same is true of shortcake and steamed puddings. In addition to either of these, the supper menu will probably include cheese and crackers, celery hearts, fruit and cookies, and maybe pie. (Pies are our greatest and best desserts, and will be covered in the following chapter.)

CHERRY PUDDING

(Serves 6)

½ cup butter
1 cup sugar
½ cup milk
¼ teaspoon salt
2 cups flour
4 teaspoons baking
   powder

1½ cups canned pie
   cherries, drained
2 tablespoons sugar
milk or cream

Cream together the butter and sugar until light. Blend in the milk alternately with the dry ingredients that have been sifted together. Put into a 6×10-inch baking dish. Put cherries over the top, sprinkling them with 2 tablespoons sugar. Bake 35 minutes in 350° oven. Serve hot with milk or cream.

SNOW PUDDING

(Serves 8)

GELATIN PART:

1 tablespoon gelatin
¼ cup cold water
1 cup boiling water

1 cup sugar
¼ cup lemon juice
3 egg whites

SOFT CUSTARD:

2 cups milk
3 egg yolks
¼ cup sugar

⅛ teaspoon salt
1 teaspoon vanilla

Soak gelatin in cold water for 5 minutes and then dissolve in the boiling water. Add sugar and lemon juice, stirring until sugar is dissolved. Cool. When thick enough to hold mark of spoon, beat until frothy. Beat egg whites until stiff and fold into lemon mixture. Continue beating until well mixed. Chill for several hours. Serve with soft custard made as follows:

Scald milk in top of double boiler. Meanwhile, beat egg yolks until thick, adding sugar and salt. Pour half of scalded milk over beaten yolks and mix well. Return to double boiler and cook over hot water until mixture coats spoon. Flavor with vanilla. Cool. To serve, pour over individual servings of gelatin.

FRUIT PUDDINGS

(Serves 4 to 6)

Made on top of the stove.

2 cups canned raspberries, cherries, or huckleberries	2 teaspoons baking powder
	¼ teaspoon salt
1 tablespoon sugar	2 egg yolks, beaten
1½ tablespoons butter	¼ cup milk
1 cup flour	cream

Put fruit into a saucepan that has a tight-fitting lid. Bring to a boil. In a bowl, cream together the sugar and butter. Add the flour, baking powder, and salt that have been sifted together. Stir in the beaten yolks and milk. Beat well. Drop from a tablespoon onto the boiling berries. Cover tightly and cook over low heat for 30 minutes. Serve with cream.

CRACKER PUDDING

(Serves 8)

My favorite pudding!

1 quart milk	1 cup sugar
15 soda crackers or	2 egg yolks, beaten
saltines, crushed	1 teaspoon vanilla extract
½ cup coconut	4 tablespoons sugar
½ teaspoon salt	2 beaten egg whites

Put the first 5 ingredients into a 2-quart saucepan and heat to almost boiling. (The crackers are crushed but not as fine as crumbs.) Pour about a cup of this hot mixture over the egg yolks. After blending together, return to pudding mixture in saucepan and cook until mixture begins to thicken, stirring all the while. Add vanilla. Pour into buttered baking dish. Cover with meringue made by folding sugar into beaten egg whites. Beat again until meringue stands in peaks. Brown in 325° oven for 20 minutes. Chill.

CUSTARD RICE PUDDING

(Serves 8)

¼ cup rice (not	1 teaspoon cinnamon
precooked)	1 teaspoon salt
6 eggs	1 cup sugar
1½ teaspoons vanilla	1 quart milk

Put rice in a small saucepan with just enough water to cover. Simmer until water evaporates.

Using a large bowl, beat the eggs. Add remaining ingredients and beat again. Add rice and stir. Pour into buttered baking dish (2-quart size) and bake 1 hour in a 325° oven.

RICE PUDDING I

(Serves 4)

This one is made with cooked rice, baked in a custard.

2 eggs	*½ teaspoon salt*
2 cups milk	*2 cups cooked rice*
⅓ cup sugar	

Beat the eggs and add ingredients in the order given. Pour into a 6×10-inch buttered baking dish. Bake 30 minutes in 350° oven.

RICE PUDDING II (With meringue)

(Serves 6)

¼ cup rice	*3 tablespoons sugar*
1 cup water	*1 teaspoon vanilla*
2 cups milk	*2 egg whites*
2 egg yolks	*4 tablespoons sugar*
⅛ teaspoon salt	

Cook rice and water in top of double boiler for about a half hour until rice swells and is dry. Add milk and keep over the boiling water for another 5 minutes. Meanwhile, beat yolks with salt and sugar. Pour some of hot milk over beaten yolks and mix well. Return egg and milk mixture to rest of hot milk. Cook over direct medium heat until creamy, about 10 minutes. Add vanilla.

Pour into baking dish and top with meringue made by beating eggs whites until frothy, then folding in sugar and beating until meringue stands in peaks. Brown in 325° oven for 20 minutes. Chill.

Note: If desired without meringue, the beaten egg whites can be folded into the creamy cooked pudding.

CREAMY RICE PUDDING
(Serves 6 to 8)

This one is distinctly different from the rice custards that contain eggs.

4 tablespoons rice (not precooked)	¼ teaspoon salt
	1 cup seedless raisins
1 quart milk	cinnamon
3 tablespoons sugar	

Rinse the rice in cold water several times. Put into a buttered 2-quart baking dish with the milk. Add sugar, salt, and raisins. Stir well. Sprinkle cinnamon over the top. Bake in 325° oven for 1 hour, stirring every 15 minutes.

CREAM PUDDING WITH CHOCOLATE MERINGUE
(Serves 6)

3 cups milk	yolks of 3 eggs, beaten
¾ cup sugar	1 tablespoon butter
4 tablespoons flour	1 teaspoon vanilla

Combine 2½ cups milk with the sugar in a 1½-quart saucepan. Warm over medium heat. Make a smooth paste with the flour and remaining milk. Add paste to beaten egg yolks.

Pour part of hot milk into egg mixture and mix well. Return to stove and, stirring constantly, cook over medium heat until pudding thickens. Add butter and vanilla. Turn into baking dish and top with Chocolate Meringue.*

CHOCOLATE MERINGUE

1 ounce melted chocolate
3 egg whites
4 tablespoons sugar

Melt chocolate and set aside. Beat egg whites until foamy. Gradually add the sugar, beating until the whites stand in peaks. Add the chocolate and beat again. Put on top of pudding. Bake 15 minutes at 350°. Chill.

CORNSTARCH WITH RASPBERRIES

(Serves 5)

A hot pudding served with chilled raspberries.

3 tablespoons cornstarch   *1 teaspoon vanilla*
⅓ cup sugar   *1 egg, beaten*
½ teaspoon salt   *1 cup canned*
2 cups milk   *raspberries*

In a 2-quart saucepan combine cornstarch, sugar, and salt. Gradually add the milk. Bring to a boil over medium heat, stirring constantly. Add vanilla. Pour part of this hot pudding over beaten egg. Return to heat with pudding for just 1 minute more, again stirring. Pour into fruit saucers. Serve warm. Top with chilled raspberries.

PAP

(*Brei*)

(Serves 4)

This is the unsweetened pudding that oldsters talk about. According to them, Pap was served so often in some homes that they feel justified in saying, "We grew up on Pap." Others claim that mothers fed it to children with the first sign of an ache or pain. For some reason, the present generation of mothers no longer relies on Pap as an indispensable food, in or out of the sickroom.

2 tablespoons flour	*1 egg, beaten*
½ teaspoon salt	*butter*
2 cups milk	*brown sugar*

Measure flour and salt into a bowl. Combine milk with beaten egg in another bowl. Add milk and egg very slowly, a little at a time, to the flour, beating all the while until smooth. Heat and boil until thickened. Pour into 4 fruit saucers and top with butter and brown sugar to taste. Serve hot.

BREAD PUDDING

(Serves 6)

2 eggs	*1 teaspoon vanilla*
2 cups milk	*4 slices bread*
½ cup sugar	*cinnamon*

In a medium-size buttered baking bowl, beat eggs. Add milk, sugar, and vanilla, and stir. Cube bread and add to egg mixture. Stir slightly. Sprinkle with cinnamon. Bake 45 minutes in 350° oven. Serve hot or cold, with or without cream.

BREAD PUDDING WITH APPLES

(Serves 4)

4 slices bread	¼ teaspoon cinnamon
¾ cup hot milk	¼ teaspoon nutmeg
2 tablespoons butter	½ cup raisins
2 eggs	1 apple, pared and diced
¼ teaspoon salt	¼ cup brown sugar
⅓ cup sugar	

Toast bread and cut into cubes. Put into buttered casserole. Cover with hot milk and dots of butter. Let bread soak for 20 minutes.

Beat eggs. Add remaining ingredients except brown sugar. Combine with bread. Pour brown sugar over the top. Bake in 300° oven for 40 minutes.

BAKED APPLE TAPIOCA

(Serves 6)

½ cup tapioca	¼ teaspoon salt
4 cups hot water	¼ teaspoon cinnamon
pinch salt	1 tablespoon butter
6 tart apples	milk or cream
1 cup sugar	

Combine first 3 ingredients in top of double boiler and cook over hot water for 15 minutes.

Pare apples and place in buttered 2-quart baking bowl. Cover with sugar, salt, cinnamon, and butter. Pour tapioca sauce over apples. Bake 30 minutes at 350° or until apples are tender. Serve with milk or cream.

PEACH TAPIOCA

(Serves 8)

A delicious ice cream sauce if you omit meringue.

4 cups sliced fresh	*3 tablespoons tapioca*
peaches	*3 egg whites*
1 cup sugar	*4 tablespoons sugar*

Put sliced peaches in a 1½-quart baking bowl. Cover with sugar and tapioca that have been mixed together. Stir to mix, then let stand for 15 minutes. Bake 45 minutes in 400° oven.

Remove pudding from oven and top with meringue that has been made by beating the egg whites and sugar together. Return to oven for another 5 minutes or until the meringue is browned.

HUCKLEBERRY PUDDING

(Serves 6)

Huckleberries grow wild in the Pennsylvania hills. They are much smaller than blueberries, but the latter can be substituted in any huckleberry recipe.

1 tablespoon butter	*2 cups huckleberries*
¾ cup sugar	*1 tablespoon flour*
1 egg, beaten	*½ cup water*
1½ cups flour	*milk or cream*
2 teaspoons baking	
powder	

Cream together the butter and sugar. Add the beaten egg. Sift together the flour and baking powder and add to the creamed mixture. Coat the huckleberries with the tablespoon of flour and add to mixture. Stir in the water.

Bake in a greased baking dish (6×10 inches) for 25 to 30 minutes in 350° oven. Serve warm with milk or cream.

GRANDMOTHER'S STEAMED PUDDING

(Serves 4 to 6)

Grandmother's Steamed Puddings were a treat that no one else could match. How well I remember the day when I asked her for the recipe and she informed me that she didn't have one, but "mixed it together just so." But further questioning soon revealed the secret. It was the long 4-hour steaming that produced the brown pudding, which didn't contain one bit of whole wheat or graham flour, or any other ingredient that would darken a pudding. My curiosity was satisfied.

In Pennsylvania Dutch country, Steamed Puddings, like Apple Dumplings,* are served as main dishes for the evening meal.

2 cups sifted flour	*2 tablespoons lard*
4 teaspoons baking	*1 egg, beaten*
powder	*½ cup milk*
½ teaspoon salt	*additional milk*
4 tablespoons sugar	

Sift together the flour, baking powder, salt, and sugar. Cut into it the lard until mixture is crumbly. Add the beaten egg and ½ cup milk and mix thoroughly.

Enclose dough in a clean white floured cloth and place in a colander over boiling water. Cover tightly and steam over low heat for 4 hours. Serve with plenty of milk.

Note: For variation, add 1 cup cherries or raisins to the dough before steaming.

ESTELLE'S STEAMED PUDDING

(Serves 4 to 6)

This is a richer pudding than the one above, having more eggs in it. If you are lucky enough to have an antique black iron kettle, be sure to use it to steam your puddings. Short steaming in any pot is satisfactory, but will not give the "brown flavor" of a pudding steamed for 4 hours.

2 tablespoons butter	3 eggs, well beaten
2½ tablespoons sugar	¾ cup milk
2 cups flour	1 cup raisins
3 teaspoons baking powder	sugar and cream

Cream together the butter and sugar. Stir in the flour and baking powder that have been sifted together. Gradually add the combined eggs and milk. Beat until smooth. Fold in the raisins.

Pour into a floured cloth or bag. Place in a colander over boiling water and steam 35 minutes. Serve with sugar and cream.

APPLE POTPIE

(Serves 6)

Here is another pie in a pot, but a dessert this time. If you are doubtful as to the goodness of Apple Potpie, try to imagine the taste of apples caramelized in brown sugar and butter. With potpie squares, this makes a delightful and unusual dessert. Heavy on calories, though!

2 cups flour
½ teaspoon salt
1 teaspoon baking
   powder
2 tablespoons lard
1 egg, beaten

⅓ cup water
6 tart apples
½ cup brown sugar
3 tablespoons butter
cream

Combine the flour, salt, and baking powder by sifting together. Into it cut the lard, until it is in tiny pieces the size of peas. Lightly stir in the beaten egg and water. On floured board, roll out as thinly as possible. Cut into 2-inch squares with knife or pastry wheel.

Pare, core, and quarter the apples. Put a layer of sliced apples and half of the brown sugar and butter into a kettle containing 1 cup water. Cover with a layer of potpie squares and then more apples, continuing until all of the apples and dough have been used. Cover tightly and steam for 20 minutes. Serve with cream.

SNOW ICE CREAM

(Serves 1)

Yes, the ice cream is made with honest-to-goodness snow! This is probably the first food that I learned to "cook." With every snow that falls, youngsters hope that it will be deep enough for two things: sledding and snow ice cream.

2 tablespoons sugar
½ teaspoon vanilla

2 cups fresh, clean snow
¼ cup milk or cream

Add the sugar and vanilla to the snow. Slowly add the milk, a little at a time. Eat immediately.

HOMEMADE ICE CREAM

(*Vanilla Flavor*)

(Serves 4)

3¼ cups cream
1 cup milk
1¼ cups sugar
1 tablespoon vanilla

10 pounds crushed ice
4 cups freezing salt
   (approximately)

Mix first 4 ingredients and pour into a 2-quart freezer can. Mix crushed ice with coarse freezing salt, using about 5 parts ice to 1 part salt. Pack ice solidly around can and to top of freezer. Turn crank slowly at first until cream begins to freeze. Crank faster until cranking becomes difficult, then remove lid and take out paddle. Cover again. Repack ice and let freezer stand at least an hour to ripen ice cream. Cover freezer with a thick layer of newspapers and a rug or blanket.

BAKED APPLE DUMPLINGS

(Serves 6)

Pastry for Two-Crust
   Pie*
3 large baking apples
6 teaspoons sugar

cinnamon
3 tablespoons butter
milk

Roll out ¾ of pastry as for pies. Cut into fourths, also as you would cut a pie. Pare and core apples and cut in half. Place an apple half on each section of pastry, cut side up. Over each apple put 1 teaspoon sugar, a dash of cinnamon, and ½ tablespoon butter. Bring up edges of dough around apple. Press around top of apple but leave opening for steam to escape. Cut off unnecessary corners of dough and add to un-used pastry. Place dumplings in baking dish.

Roll out rest of dough and make other dumplings. Bake in 350° oven 20 to 30 minutes or until apples are soft. Serve with milk.

BOILED APPLE DUMPLINGS
(Serves 6)

2 cups flour	¾ cup milk
4 teaspoons baking powder	3 large tart apples
½ teaspoon salt	6 teaspoons sugar
2 tablespoons sugar	milk
2 tablespoons vegetable shortening	sugar

Sift together the flour, baking powder, salt, and sugar. Cut in the shortening until it is the size of peas. Stir in the milk. On a floured board, roll dough to ½-inch thickness. Cut into 6 squares.

Pare and core apples and cut in halves. Put a half on each square of dough and one teaspoon sugar on each apple. Pull the 4 corners of the dough together, dampen slightly, and press to seal. Tie each dumpling in a clean piece of white muslin.

Drop dumplings into a large kettle of boiling water. Cook 20 to 25 minutes, depending upon the size of the apple. Serve in soup dishes with milk and additional sugar if desired.

PEACH UPSIDEDOWN CAKE
(Serves 6)

Prepare like Rhubarb Upsidedown Cake,* but substitute canned peaches for the rhubarb and use half the amount of brown sugar.

RHUBARB UPSIDEDOWN CAKE

(Serves 6)

2½ cups rhubarb, cut in
  ½-inch pieces
1 cup brown sugar
2 cups flour, unsifted
½ teaspoon salt
4 tablespoons sugar

4 teaspoons baking
  powder
¼ cup shortening
1 egg
¾ cup milk
additional milk

Put rhubarb into a buttered 9-inch cake pan. Cover with the brown sugar.

Sift together the flour, salt, sugar, and baking powder. Cut the shortening into the dry ingredients with a pastry blender or 2 knives until the mixture has the consistency of very coarse corn meal. Beat the egg, then add the milk to it. Carefully stir the egg and milk mixture into the dry ingredients. Beat vigorously for 10 seconds. Spoon dough over the sugared rhubarb and then spread evenly.

Bake in 350° oven for 35 minutes. Cut into 6 wedges and serve warm with milk.

Pies

Where does one begin to talk about Pennsylvania Dutch pies? What is most unusual about them—their quality, quantity, or variety? A difficult question, because we excel in all three.

Pennsylvania Dutch cooks turn out good pies because they are experienced in pie baking and know that one uses plenty of butter, eggs, nuts, and cream to produce the best pies. As for the pastry, they are so adept that they know "by the feel of it" how much water to add. All are pie bakers, but the farmer's wife produces the greatest quantities. For those who baked in the outdoor Dutch ovens, it was customary to slide fifteen pies into the oven at one time.

What about variety? Practically everything under the sun is put into pies. We make meat pies, vegetable pies, fruit pies, molasses pies, cream pies, and milk pies. By far the most popular of these is the Shoo-Fly Pie.* Its popularity is partially due to its flavor and partially to the fact that it retains its freshness longer than any other pie.

The curious name of this dessert has intrigued many a folklore student, but none have authenticated its origin. According to Dr. Preston Barba and Ann Hark, co-authors of *Pennsylvania German Cookery,* "It has been suggested that it is a corruption of the French *choufleur* (cauliflower), since the texture of its crumb-besprinkled surface resembles a head of cauliflower. . . . More important than the name is the baking." Then again, it could have been named shoo-fly because its sweetness attracted the flies.

There are many variations in shoo-fly pies—in texture, flavor, and the procedure used in making them. Sometimes the molasses mixture is poured into the pastry and topped with crumbs, while other times the liquid and crumbs are alternated or even mixed.

Although there are half a dozen different kinds of lemon pies, and Lemon Strip Pie* is the most unusual because it has molasses in the filling and a cookie dough for the topping. Mc-Kinley Cake Pie* also has lemon flavoring but is not generally included in the category of lemon pies. Milk Pie* is just a little thin pie that is made from leftover pastry, and yet its story is much too big to tell here. Its popularity makes it deserving of a separate story which is told at the end of this chapter.

PASTRY FOR PIE SHELL

1½ cups sifted
  all-purpose flour
½ teaspoon salt

½ cup lard (vegetable
  shortening can be used
  but lard is preferred
  by Pennsylvania
  Dutch cooks)
3 or 4 tablespoons cold
  water

PASTRY FOR TWO-CRUST PIE

2¼ cups sifted
  all-purpose flour
1 teaspoon salt

¾ cup shortening (lard
  is preferred)
4 or 5 tablespoons
  cold water

METHOD FOR MAKING PASTRY:

Combine sifted flour and salt in mixing bowl. Cut in the lard or shortening with 2 knives or pastry blender until the shortening is the size of little peas. Sprinkle on the cold water, a tablespoon at a time, tossing and mixing lightly with a fork, adding the water to the driest crumbs.

Shape dough with hands into a ball (2 balls if making 2 crusts). Roll on lightly floured surface, with floured rolling pin. Roll dough lightly from center to edges in all directions to make a circle 1 inch larger than pan. Pastry should be about ⅛ inch thick. To lift pastry into pan use rolling pin, rolling dough over rolling pin. Gently fit crust, taking care not to stretch dough. Trim edge even with piepan. Before baking unfilled shells, prick with fork to allow steam to escape. Bake 10 minutes at 425°.

CRUMBS FOR PIE TOPPING

(9-inch fruit pies)

¾ *cup flour*
⅓ *cup butter or margarine*
½ *cup sugar*

Using your fingers, mix together the flour, butter, and sugar until they are fine crumbs. Spread evenly over fruit fillings in unbaked pastry shells. Bake 10 minutes at 425°, then 30 minutes longer at 350°.

SHOO-FLY PIE I

(3 7-inch pies)

The dry kind—good for dunking. There is a Shoo-Fly Pie to suit every taste: dry, moist, and in-between! The kind of molasses used is up to the individual. Some like to use baking molasses, others prefer table molasses, and a third group uses a mixture of the two. Where the old barrel molasses is available, Pennsylvania Dutch cooks use that.

1 cup molasses   *1 cup brown sugar*
1 cup boiling water   *¾ cup lard*
1 teaspoon baking soda   *3 Pastry Shells,**
4 cups flour (unsifted)   *unbaked*

Mix the molasses and boiling water. Cool slightly, then add the baking soda. While it is cooling, mix the crumbs:

With fingers, work flour, brown sugar, and lard into crumbs. Pour the molasses mixture into unbaked crusts. Top with the crumbs. Bake 25 minutes at 350°.

~~~~~~

SHOO-FLY PIE II

(1 9-inch pie)

This one has a "damp zone" next to the crust. It is sometimes referred to as the "wet-bottom shoo-fly." Most people
prefer this one above the others.

1 egg yolk	*⅛ teaspoon ginger*
½ cup molasses	*⅛ teaspoon cloves*
¾ cup boiling water	*½ cup brown sugar*
1 teaspoon baking soda	*½ teaspoon salt*
1 cup flour	*2 tablespoons shortening*
½ teaspoon cinnamon	*Pastry Shell,* unbaked*
⅛ teaspoon nutmeg	

Beat the egg yolk in a small bowl. Blend in the molasses.
Add the boiling water with the soda dissolved in it. Set aside.
Combine dry ingredients with shortening and work into
crumbs with fingers. Put liquid into pastry shell and top with
crumbs. Bake in a 400° oven for 10 minutes, then reduce heat
to 325° and bake 35 minutes longer.

SHOO-FLY PIE III

(9-inch pie)

This is the cake type. The liquid and crumbs are combined
before baking. Or, as some cooks do, the crumbs and liquid
can be put into the crust alternately.

1½ cups flour	*2 tablespoons shortening*
½ cup brown sugar	*½ cup hot water*
½ cup white sugar	*¾ teaspoon baking soda*
1 teaspoon baking	*½ cup molasses*
* powder*	*Pastry Shell,* unbaked*

In a large bowl combine the flour, sugars, baking powder, and shortening by working into crumbs with fingers. Set aside.

Mix together the hot water, baking soda, and molasses. Add this liquid to the crumbs and mix slightly. Pour into unbaked pastry shell. Bake in a moderate oven, 350°, for 40 minutes.

MOLASSES COCONUT CUSTARD I

(1 9-inch pie)

Sometimes Sweet Dough* strips are put on this pie. It is then called *Hussa Drayer Kucha* (Suspender Cake).

2 tablespoons flour	1 cup milk
½ teaspoon baking soda	½ cup cream, sweet or
1 cup sugar	sour
2 eggs	1 cup coconut
1 cup table molasses or	Pastry Shell,* unbaked
Karo syrup	

Combine the flour, soda, and sugar. Beat the eggs and add with the molasses to the dry ingredients. Add the milk, cream, and coconut, stirring after each addition. Bake in the pie shell for 50 minutes at 350°.

MOLASSES COCONUT CUSTARD II

(1 9-inch pie)

Not as sweet as Molasses Coconut Custard I.

½ teaspoon soda	2 tablespoons flour
½ cup buttermilk	½ cup molasses
1 egg, beaten	½ cup coconut
½ cup sour cream	Pastry Shell,* unbaked
½ cup sugar	

Dissolve the soda in the buttermilk and set aside. Combine the egg and sour cream, then stir in the sugar and flour that have been mixed together. Add the molasses and buttermilk and beat until blended. Stir in the coconut.

Pour into unbaked shell. Bake 40 minutes in 350° oven.

QUAKERTOWN PIES

(2 9-inch pies)

Very similar to the shoo-fly. They must be first cousins. It is more gooey than the moist shoo-fly.

1 cup brown sugar	2 cups flour, unsifted
3 tablespoons flour	¼ cup lard
½ cup molasses	¼ cup butter
1 egg, beaten	1 cup brown sugar
2 cups hot water	Pastry for 2 Pie Shells,*
1 teaspoon baking soda	unbaked

In a quart-size saucepan mix the sugar, flour, molasses, beaten egg, and hot water. Bring to a boil. Remove from heat and stir in the baking soda. Cool.

In a bowl mix together with your hands the next 4 ingredients, making fine crumbs. Put molasses mixture into the pastry shells and cover with crumbs. Bake in 350° oven for 30 to 35 minutes.

MOLASSES PIE

(1 9-inch pie)

This is like a cake in a pie shell. If only we could have eaten this instead of that awful combination of molasses and sulphur that we used to be given each spring. It seems to me

that we were told that it would thin our blood. I don't suppose
Molasses Pie can do that.

½ cup sugar
¾ cup flour
2 tablespoons butter
¼ cup boiling water

¼ cup New Orleans
   baking molasses
¼ teaspoon baking soda
Pastry Shell,* unbaked

With your fingers, work the sugar, flour, and butter together
until the mixture is crumbly. Beat the water, molasses, and soda
together. Combine the liquid with the dry ingredients but do
not beat. Turn into an unbaked pastry shell. Bake for 30 minutes at 325°.

MONTGOMERY PIES

(3 8-inch pies)

The requests that I have had for this recipe have outnumbered
all other requests for pie recipes. All these persons have been
looking for "a pie that Grandma used to make, called Mont-
gomery Pie." It is a lemon-flavored molasses custard with a
cake-like top.

Pastry for 3 Pie Shells*
2½ cups flour
3 teaspoons baking
   powder
2 cups sugar
½ cup butter and lard,
   mixed
2 eggs, beaten
1 cup milk

1 egg, beaten
grated rind and juice of
   1 lemon
1 cup sugar
2 teaspoons flour
1 cup water
1 cup molasses or Blue
   Label Karo

Line piepans with pastry.

Sift together the flour and baking powder. Set aside. Cream together the sugar and shortening. Add beaten eggs and mix well. Add the sifted flour and milk alternately. Set aside while you make liquid for lower part of pies.

To the beaten egg add the grated rind and juice of the lemon, the sugar, and flour, beating well. Slowly stir in the water and molasses. Pour this into the 3 pastry shells. Spoon first mixture over liquid.

Bake at 350° for 35 to 40 minutes.

MCKINLEY CAKE PIES

(3 8-inch pies)

1 tablespoon flour	2 eggs, beaten
1 cup sugar	1 cup milk
grated rind and juice of	2½ cups flour
1 lemon	1½ teaspoons baking
1 egg, beaten	powder
1 cup molasses	½ teaspoon salt
2 cups hot water	3 Pastry Shells,*
2 cups sugar	unbaked
½ cup lard	

Combine the flour and sugar. Add the grated rind and juice of the lemon. Stir in the beaten egg and molasses. Slowly stir in the hot water. Set aside.

Cream together the sugar and lard. Stir in the beaten eggs. Alternately add the milk and the dry ingredients that have been sifted together.

Divide liquid mixture into the 3 pastry shells. Spoon batter over the top. Bake 35 minutes at 375°.

UNION PIES

(2 9-inch pies)

1 cup sugar	*1 cup sour cream*
5 tablespoons flour	*2 cups buttermilk*
1 teaspoon baking soda	*2 Pastry Shells,**
1 egg, beaten	*unbaked*
1 cup molasses or Blue	
Label Karo	

Mix together the first 3 ingredients. Add beaten egg. Add remaining ingredients in the order given, mixing well after each addition. (Buttermilk should be added slowly.) Pour into unbaked shells and bake for 35 minutes at 375°.

SUGAR PIE

(1 9-inch pie)

½ cup sugar	*1 small egg, beaten*
¾ cup flour	*¼ cup milk*
1 tablespoon butter	*⅛ teaspoon salt*
1 tablespoon lard	*1 tablespoon lemon juice*
2 teaspoons baking	*Pastry Shell,** unbaked*
powder	

With your fingers, work the mixture of sugar, flour, butter, and lard into fine crumbs. Set aside ¼ cup for top crumbs. To the remainder of crumbs add the baking powder, beaten egg, milk, salt, and lemon juice. Mix well and turn into unbaked pastry shell. Top with reserved crumbs. Bake for 35 minutes at 375°.

~~~~~~

AMISH VANILLA PIES

(2 9-inch pies)

Here is another cousin to the Shoo-Fly Pie.* Like the Quaker-town,* it is more gooey than the wet-bottom shoo-fly. At the famous Lancaster Farmers' Markets, Vanilla Pies are best sellers, available from the Amish women who bake them.

1 cup sugar	*1 cup brown sugar*
4 tablespoons flour	*1 teaspoon cream of*
1 egg, well beaten	*tartar*
1 cup molasses or Blue	*1 teaspoon baking soda*
Label Karo	*¼ cup butter*
2 cups water	*¼ cup lard*
1 teaspoon vanilla	*2 Pastry Shells,**
2 cups flour	*unbaked*

Combine the first 6 ingredients in a saucepan in the order given. Bring to a full rolling boil, then set aside to cool. Put remaining ingredients into a large bowl and rub together with fingers to make crumbs.

Pour ½ of cooked mixture into each unbaked pastry shell. Cover with crumbs. Bake 40 to 45 minutes at 350°.

COCONUT CUSTARD PIE

(2 pies, or 1 pie and 4 cups custard)

*Pastry for 2 Pie Shells**	*1 teaspoon vanilla*
3 eggs	*½ teaspoon salt*
¾ cup sugar	*3 ounces moist shredded*
3 cups milk	*coconut*

Line 2 9-inch piepans with pastry.

Beat eggs slightly with a fork. Add all the remaining ingredients and mix well. Pour into unbaked pie shells and bake 10 minutes in a 450° oven, then 35 minutes more at 325°. Test with a silver knife: if custard does not adhere to knife, it is fully baked.

WHITE COCONUT CUSTARD

(2 8-inch custards)

This should have been called "Heavenly Custard"—it is that delicious. It is made with fresh grated coconut.

2 Pastry Shells,* baked
1 cup sugar
5 tablespoons cornstarch
3 cups milk

1 teaspoon vanilla
1 coconut, grated
2 egg whites, beaten stiff

Roll out pastry and line 2 piepans.

In a saucepan mix the sugar and cornstarch. Gradually add the milk. Cook over medium heat until thickened, stirring constantly, as it scorches easily. Add vanilla and ¾ of the coconut. Cool 15 minutes. Fold in stiffly beaten egg whites. Put custard into pie shells and cover with remaining coconut. Place in 450° oven for a few minutes to brown coconut.

BUTTERSCOTCH PIE

(1 9-inch pie)

3 tablespoons butter
⅔ cup light brown sugar
5 tablespoons flour
2 beaten egg yolks
1 teaspoon vanilla

¼ teaspoon salt
2 cups hot milk
Pastry Shell,* baked
2 beaten egg whites
2 tablespoons sugar

Cream together the butter and sugar. Add the flour, egg yolks, vanilla, and salt. Add hot milk slowly. Bring to a boil, then boil 1 full minute, stirring constantly. Cool.

When cool, pour into baked pie shell. Cover with meringue made by beating whites until partially stiff, adding the sugar, and beating until stiff.

Brown meringue in a slow oven, 300°, for 15 to 20 minutes.

APPLESAUCE CUSTARD PIE

(1 9-inch pie)

3 eggs	*1½ cups applesauce*
½ cup sugar	*½ cup milk*
½ teaspoon cinnamon	*Pastry Shell,* unbaked*
¼ teaspoon salt	

Beat eggs in medium-size bowl. Mix together sugar, cinnamon, and salt and add to eggs. Beat well. Blend in applesauce and milk. Pour into unbaked crust. Bake 10 minutes at 450° and 35 minutes more at 350°.

VANILLA CUSTARD

(1 9-inch custard)

A delicious boiled custard poured into a baked crust and topped with a meringue.

½ cup cream	*¼ cup milk*
2 cups milk	*1 teaspoon vanilla*
2 egg yolks	*Pastry Shell,* baked*
1 cup sugar	*2 egg whites*
¼ cup flour	*2 tablespoons sugar*

Add cream to milk and let come to a boil. Beat egg yolks with sugar, flour, and the ¼ cup milk. Pour hot milk over egg mixture and return to heat. Stirring constantly, let boil 1 minute. Flavor with vanilla and cool.

When partially cool, pour into baked crust. Top with meringue made by beating egg whites with sugar until it stands up in peaks. Brown in 325° oven for about 12 minutes.

CHOCOLATE FUNNY CAKE PIE

(9-inch pie)

A funny cake pie because the top chocolate layer goes to the bottom!

1 cup sugar	*½ teaspoon vanilla*
¼ cup butter	*Pastry Shell,* unbaked*
½ cup milk	*4 tablespoons cocoa*
1 egg, beaten	*½ cup sugar*
1 cup flour	*6 tablespoons water*
1 teaspoon baking	*½ teaspoon vanilla*
powder	

Cream together the sugar and butter. Add the combined milk and egg alternately with flour and baking powder. Add the vanilla. Put into pastry shell.

Mix the cocoa and sugar. Add the water and vanilla gradually. Pour over cake batter. Bake in 350° oven for 35 minutes or until firm.

PUMPKIN PIE

(9-inch pie)

If ever there were any better Pumpkin Pies, the Pennsylvania Dutch would have made them. We have dozens of recipes for them. The neck pumpkins are considered the best for pies.

2 cups mashed pumpkin
1 cup milk
2 beaten egg yolks
¼ teaspoon ginger
¼ teaspoon nutmeg
¼ teaspoon cloves
1¼ teaspoons cinnamon

⅔ cup sugar
½ teaspoon salt
2 egg whites, beaten stiff
½ cup coconut
   (optional)
Pastry Shell,* unbaked

Mix together pumpkin, milk, egg yolks, and spices. Beat in sugar and salt. Fold in the stiffly beaten egg whites and coconut. Pour into unbaked shell. Bake in a very hot oven, 450°, for 10 minutes. Reduce heat to 375° and bake 20 minutes longer.

PUMPKIN CUSTARDS

(3 7-inch pies)

This one has a cooked filling that can be kept in the refrigerator for several days. Crusts can be filled just 3 hours before serving. A whipped cream topping really tops them off!

1 quart mashed pumpkin
2 cups dark brown sugar
3 tablespoons flour
1 teaspoon ginger
1 teaspoon cloves
1 teaspoon nutmeg
2 teaspoons cinnamon

1 teaspoon salt
4 eggs, well beaten
1 quart milk
2 tablespoons butter
3 Pastry Shells,* baked
whipping cream

Mix together the pumpkin, sugar, flour, spices, and salt in a large saucepan. Gradually add the eggs and milk. Boil mixture until thick, stirring constantly. Add butter and stir until melted. When cool, store in covered container in refrigerator or put into baked pie shells immediately. Spread whipped cream over the top. Refrigerate for 3 hours.

WALNUT CUSTARD

(9-inch custard)

1½ cups sugar
3 tablespoons flour
2 eggs, beaten
1 cup black walnut
    kernels
½ cup molasses

1 cup water
Pastry Shell,* unbaked
1 cup whipping cream
½ teaspoon vanilla
2 teaspoons sugar

Mix together the sugar and flour. Add beaten eggs. Put nuts through nut chopper or coarse-food chopper, then add to mixture. Slowly stir in molasses and water. Pour into unbaked pastry shell. Bake in 375° oven for 5 minutes. Reducing heat to 325°, bake 30 minutes more. Chill. To serve, top with whipped cream that has been flavored and sweetened.

SHELLBARK CUSTARDS

(2 9-inch pies)

Shellbarks are hickory nuts that make this a dream pie! A very thin layer of filling is made because the pie is so rich.

1 cup shellbark or
    hickory kernels, rolled
    fine
1 cup sugar
3 tablespoons cornstarch
1 egg

1 cup molasses
1 cup water
¼ teaspoon salt
2 Pastry Shells,* baked
1 cup whipping cream

In a quart-size saucepan, combine nuts, sugar, and cornstarch. Beat the egg and add to it the molasses, water, and salt.

Blend well. Slowly add to the sugar and nuts. Boil until thickened, stirring all the while. Cool. Pour into baked crusts. Top with whipped cream. Chill several hours before serving.

GREEN TOMATO PIE

(9-inch pie)

Pastry for 2-Crust Pie
green tomatoes, about
  2 pounds
¼ teaspoon salt
1 teaspoon cinnamon
¼ teaspoon ginger

2 tablespoons flour
½ cup brown sugar
½ cup molasses or Blue
  Karo syrup
2 tablespoons butter

Roll out ½ of pastry on floured board and line piepan. Slice unpeeled green tomatoes in ¼-inch slices and measure 3 cups. Arrange slices in pastry shell and season with salt and spices. Sprinkle flour over tomatoes and cover with brown sugar and molasses. Dot with butter and cover with top crust.

Bake 10 minutes at 425° and then 35 minutes more at 350°.

FRUIT CUSTARD PIE

(9-inch custard)

This is the basic recipe for fresh fruit custards, but canned fruit can be substituted.

4 peaches or 2 cups
  raspberries or cherries
Pastry Shell, unbaked*
2 eggs

¾ cup sugar
1 cup milk
1 tablespoon butter
cinnamon

Slice peeled peaches into bottom of pastry shell, or spread cherries or raspberries over bottom. Beat eggs and sugar thoroughly. Add milk and pour over fruit. Dot with butter and sprinkle with cinnamon.

Bake 10 minutes at 425°, then reduce heat to 350° and bake 30 minutes longer. Serve chilled.

PEACH CREAM PIE

(9-inch custard)

3 or 4 peaches	*¾ cup sugar*
Pastry Shell, unbaked*	*¾ cup coffee cream*
3 teaspoons flour	*cinnamon*

Peel peaches and cut into halves. Lay them in pastry shell, round side up. Cover with flour and sugar mixed together. Add cream. Sprinkle lightly with cinnamon.

Bake in hot oven, 425°, for 10 minutes, then 325° for 35 minutes.

CHERRY CRUMB PIE

(9-inch pie)

2 cups cherry pie filling	*⅓ cup butter*
Pastry Shell, unbaked*	*½ cup sugar*
¾ cup flour	

Put cherry pie filling into shell. Mix the flour, butter, and sugar with fingers until they are fine crumbs. Pour over cherries. Bake 10 minutes at 425°, then 30 minutes at 350°.

FRESH PEACH CRUMB PIE

(9-inch pie)

The Pennsylvania Dutch make as many crumb-topped fruit pies as two-crust pies.

1 cup sugar
2½ tablespoons
   cornstarch
¼ teaspoon salt
½ cup water

4 cups sliced peaches
   (about 6)
1 tablespoon lemon juice
Crumbs for Pie
   Topping*
Pastry Shell,* unbaked

In a saucepan combine sugar, cornstarch, and salt. Add water and peaches and bring to a boil. Boil 1 minute. Add lemon juice and cool.

Meanwhile, make crumbs. Put peaches into pastry shell. Cover with crumbs. Bake 10 minutes in 450° oven, then 20 minutes more at 375°.

SOUR CREAM APPLE TART

(9-inch tart)

Open-faced pies are called tarts. Apple pies are also made with two crusts or with crumbs. It is the favorite fruit pie of this regional cookery. Stayman Winesap apples are preferred for pies.

Pastry for Pie Shell,*
   unbaked
1 cup sour cream
¾ cup sugar
2 tablespoons flour
¼ teaspoon salt

1 teaspoon vanilla
1 egg
2 cups diced tart apples
⅓ cup brown sugar
⅓ cup flour
¼ cup butter

Line piepan with pastry. Beat together sour cream, sugar, flour, salt, vanilla, and egg. Add the diced apples and pour mixture into piepan.

Bake in 400° oven for 25 minutes. Remove from oven and cover with crumbs that have been made by mixing together the brown sugar, flour, and butter. Return to oven and bake for 20 minutes more.

DUTCH APPLE TART

(9-inch tart)

8 medium-size apples	*1 tablespoon butter*
¼ cup sugar	*¼ teaspoon nutmeg*
1 tablespoon flour	*¾ cup sugar*
Pastry Shell,* unbaked	

Peel and core apples. Slice into a bowl and mix sugar and flour with them. Turn into the unbaked crust. Dot with butter and sprinkle with nutmeg. Cover with sugar. Bake 45 minutes at 350°.

SCHNITZ PIE

(9-inch pie)

Tart apples are dried for winter schnitz pies. This same recipe is used to make individual half-moon pies that are carried in lunch boxes.

2 cups dried sour apples	*½ teaspoon cinnamon*
1½ cups water	*Pastry for 2-Crust Pie**
¾ cup sugar	

Soak dried apples (*schnitz*) overnight in the water. Cook them in this same water. When soft, put through colander or mash thoroughly. Add sugar and cinnamon. Turn into pastry-lined pan and top with crust.

Bake for 10 minutes at 425°, then reduce heat to 350° and bake 30 minutes longer.

RASPBERRY CUSTARD

(8-inch custard)

Bright in color, full of flavor, and never a seed to spoil it! This is one of the most delicious tarts that one can make. And so easily! Do you know what we do with the leftover raspberries? We serve them, chilled, over hot cornstarch pudding.

juice from a number 2 can raspberries	*Pastry Shell,* baked*
1 tablespoon sugar	*1 cup whipping cream*
3 tablespoons cornstarch	*2 teaspoons sugar*
	½ teaspoon vanilla

Add enough water to the drained raspberry juice to make 2 cups liquid. (For full flavor, there should be at least 1½ cups juice.)

Combine sugar and cornstarch in a saucepan. Slowly add the juice to the cornstarch and sugar, stirring until smooth. Boil until thickened, stirring constantly. Cool before putting into baked pastry shell. Whip cream, adding sugar and vanilla when beating. Whip until stiff. Spoon cream over raspberry custard. Chill 3 hours before serving.

FUNERAL PIE

(9-inch pie)

'Tis nothing more than a raisin pie! It used to be served at so many funeral suppers that it got to be known as the Funeral Pie. Perhaps, as someone suggested, it was served so regularly because of its somber color. It's a good guess. Except where horse and buggy transportation is still in use among the Amish, there are not many funeral suppers served. However, we still eat raisin pies, and at more pleasurable occasions.

2 cups raisins	*2 tablespoons lemon*
1½ cups hot water	*juice*
½ cup sugar	*½ teaspoon salt*
2 tablespoons cornstarch	*1 tablespoon butter*
grated rind of ½ lemon	*Pastry for 2-Crust Pie**

Put raisins in pan with hot water and boil 5 minutes. Combine sugar and cornstarch, mixing thoroughly, and add to raisins. Stir and cook over low heat about 5 minutes longer, until thickened. Remove from heat and add lemon rind and juice, salt, and butter.

Bake between 2 crusts for 30 minutes at 375°.

LEMON STRIP PIE

(*With Sweet Dough*)

(2 9-inch pies)

Just one of the many different lemon pies we make. Among them are custards, cake pies, and two-crust pies. More popular than lemon meringue pies among the Pennsylvania Dutch is the Lemon Strip Pie, sometimes called Lemon Sponge. It has a lemon filling that is topped with strips of sweet dough, which is a cookie dough. This is sometimes cut into circles or rectangles instead of strips. Another variation is made by some who double the sweet dough recipe and use it for the base of the pie as well as the topping.

LEMON FILLING:

2 tablespoons butter	grated rind and juice of
1 cup sugar	1 lemon
3 tablespoons flour	⅞ cup Blue Label Karo
2 eggs, well beaten	1 cup cold water

Combine all the ingredients in a saucepan. Stirring constantly over medium heat, cook until mixture thickens. Set aside until the sweet dough is made.

TO MAKE SWEET DOUGH:

½ cup light brown sugar	1 teaspoon baking
¼ cup lard	powder
1 egg, beaten	1 teaspoon baking soda
1 cup flour	3 tablespoons milk

Cream together the sugar and lard. Blend in the beaten egg. Add the flour, baking powder, and baking soda which have been sifted together. Lastly, add the milk.

Roll out the dough on floured board to size of pie. Cut into strips 1 inch wide.

BOTTOM CRUST:

2 Pastry Shells,* unbaked

Pour lemon liquid into pastry-lined pans. Place parallel strips (not crisscross) over the top. Bake 30 minutes at 350°.

RHUBARB CUSTARD WITH MERINGUE

(9-inch custard)

2 beaten egg yolks	*Pastry Shell,* unbaked*
1 cup sugar	*2 tablespoons butter*
¼ teaspoon salt	*4 tablespoons sugar*
2 tablespoons flour	*2 beaten egg whites*
2 cups diced rhubarb	

Combine the beaten yolks, sugar, salt, and flour with the rhubarb. Mix well. Turn into an unbaked pastry shell. Dot with butter. Bake 35 minutes in 350° oven.

Remove from oven and top with the meringue: Add sugar gradually while beating egg whites. Continue beating until whites stand up in soft peaks. Spoon onto baked custard and return to oven for 15 minutes more to brown.

LEMON CAKE PIE

(9-inch pie)

This is the lemon pie that is popular in Lancaster County, whereas the strip pie is the favorite one in Berks County. The Lemon Cake Pie is made with one batter, but the egg whites rise to the top, forming a sort of cake topping over the lemon filling.

1 cup sugar	*grated rind and juice of*
1 tablespoon butter	*1 lemon*
2 eggs, separated	*1 cup milk*
2 tablespoons flour	*Pastry Shell,* unbaked*

Cream together the sugar and butter. Stir in beaten egg yolks, flour, grated rind, lemon juice, and milk. Fold in stiffly beaten egg whites. Pour into an unbaked pie shell and bake 10 minutes at 450°. Reduce temperature to 325° and bake for 20 minutes more.

LEMON CRUMB TARTS

(2 8-inch tarts)

If you like a strong lemon flavor, this is the one for you.

1½ cups sugar
grated rind and juice of
   2 lemons
3 eggs, beaten
1 cup boiling water
1 cup sugar

1¾ cups flour
2 teaspoons baking
   powder
3 tablespoons butter
2 Pastry Shells,*
   unbaked

Add the sugar and lemon rind and juice to the beaten eggs. Slowly stir in the boiling water. Set aside.

With fingers, work together the sugar, flour, baking powder, and butter until it is in fine crumbs. Pour lemon filling into crusts and cover with the crumbs. Bake 40 minutes at 400° or until nicely browned.

MILK PIE

(8-inch tart)

Displaced Pennsylvania Dutchmen remember Milk Pie with nostalgia. One man living in Texas searched for a Milk Pie recipe for thirty years! During that time, nieces, cousins, and daughters-in-law had tried every recipe for cream pie that they could find. When they finally found the recipe in my first cookbook, the whole family rejoiced.

Even though it is a family favorite, we consider Milk Pie much too common for guests. Actually, it is a children's pie, the one they are allowed to eat between meals. Even the cookie jar loses its attraction when there is a Milk Pie in the Dutch cupboard. It is served more often as a snack than as a dessert.

Every Pennsylvania Dutch cook knows how to make Milk Pies "by guess." Into an unbaked pastry shell she puts a giant-sized pinch of flour and an equal amount of sugar, mixing lightly with her fingers, and then covering with top milk or cream. With a sprinkling of cinnamon over the top, the pie is ready for the oven.

Milk Pie is a pie so thin that it has been called the pie with nothing in it. Since it is a by-product of baking day and is made with leftover pastry, the size of the pie varies. Sometimes there is enough pastry for a full size, but more often there is only enough for tiny four- or five-inch pies. Among these thrifty cooks, not even five inches of pie dough is to be wasted. It will be used for a milk pie, or shaped into a pretzel, or perhaps rolled and cut into cinnamon pinwheels.

4 tablespoons flour	1½ cups milk or cream
4 tablespoons sugar	dash of cinnamon
Pastry Shell,* unbaked	

Combine the flour and sugar, mixing well. Put into unbaked shell. Pour milk or cream over mixture and sprinkle with cinnamon. (Top milk was always used for this tart before homogenized milk came into use.) Bake in 350° oven for 45 minutes. Pie will be runny. For the few who like it thicker, use less milk or let the pie set a day before eating it.

Many families seem to have had pet names for this pie, with slight variations in its making. The ones who add a tablespoon of molasses or substitute brown sugar for the white, call it: Candy Pie, Goody Pie, Love Pie, or Butterscotch Pie. These, too, are names for Milk Pie: Poor Man's Pie, Cream Tart, Promise Pie, Eat-me-Quick Pie, Grandmother's Pie, Nothing Pie, Everyday Pie, Johnny Pie, Sugar Pie, Mennonite Pie, and Milich Tart. Other names for the same pie are dialect names: *Milich Flitche, Schlebby, Rawm Kawder, Schlopp Kuche, Milich Flabies,* and *Milich Schabbies.* A lot of names for a little pie that is made with leftover pastry!

Cakes, Plain and Fancy

THE old handwritten cookbooks contain more cake "receipts" than anything else. Usually these receipts list the ingredients with never a word as to method. In Grandma's time cooking directions were unnecessary, since every girl knew all about cake baking long before she was "of age."

Cake baking among the Pennsylvania Dutch is an art. To see an exhibition of prize winners, attend the Farm Show or County Fair. Spongecakes and angel foods were never any higher. The fair, however, does not surpass the triumph of the cakes at an Amish wedding. Here, neither number, size, nor beauty can be surpassed. If heavily laden tables ever groaned, it must be here where feasting lasts all day. For the occasion, cooks for miles around contribute their homemade cakes.

The first part of this chapter contains the recipes for plain cakes—the cakes without icing. All of them, with the exception of Applesauce Cake* and Sunshine Cake,* are appropriate breakfast cakes. In modern terminology, they might very well be described as coffeecakes, but the Pennsylvania Dutch do not speak of them as such. Instead, we call them dunking cakes. Most cakes in this category are crumb cakes. Our crumb pies, too, are often called *Kucha* (cake) by our own people.

The recipes in the latter part of this chapter are fancy cakes—frosted layer cakes. Included, too, is the very special one made of spongecake cones and called Morning Glory Cake.* There are other interesting ones—not the usual kind but some different ones, such as Lolly's Cake* or Blotch Kucha.*

Icing recipes are included at the end of the chapter.

SHOO-FLY CAKE

(1 9×13-inch loaf)

4 cups unsifted flour
2 cups light brown sugar
1 cup vegetable
   shortening
¼ teaspoon cinnamon

1 cup Karo syrup (Blue Label)
2 cups boiling water
1 tablespoon baking soda

Mix together the flour and sugar, then cut in the shortening to make crumbs, as for pastry. Measure out 1 cup of these crumbs to use on top of cake.

Add cinnamon to the original mixture and stir it, adding the syrup. Slowly add the boiling water, but reserve ¼ cup to dissolve baking soda. Lastly, stir in the dissolved soda.

Place in 9×13-inch loaf pan and top with crumbs. Bake 45 minutes in a 375° oven.

ADA'S APPLE CAKE

(1 9×13-inch cake)

Adapted from a handwritten receipt book dated 1850.

2 cups sifted flour
4 teaspoons baking
  powder
½ teaspoon salt
2 teaspoons sugar
3 tablespoons butter

1 egg, well beaten
¾ cup milk
6 medium apples
⅓ cup cinnamon sugar
2 tablespoons butter

Into a large bowl sift the first 4 ingredients. Add 3 tablespoons butter, and, with hands, work into crumbs. Stir in egg and milk, then beat. Spread in greased 9×13-inch pan.

Peel and core apples and cut into eighths. Put on top of the cake dough, pressing slices halfway into dough. Cover with cinnamon sugar and butter. Bake for 30 minutes at 400°. Serve hot or cold.

MILKLESS, EGGLESS, BUTTERLESS CAKE

(A 10-inch round cake)

This Moravian cake is baked in an old-fashioned cast-iron skillet. It bears a great resemblance to Applesauce Cake.*

1 cup dark brown sugar
1 cup water
1½ cups raisins
⅓ cup lard
1 teaspoon cinnamon
⅓ teaspoon cloves
¼ teaspoon salt

¼ teaspoon ground
  nutmeg
1 teaspoon baking soda
1 tablespoon warm water
2 cups sifted flour
½ teaspoon baking
  powder

Boil together the first 8 ingredients for 3 minutes. Cool. Dissolve soda in warm water. Sift together flour and baking powder. When the boiled mixture has cooled enough so that your hands can comfortably hold the side of the pan, add the soda and flour to it. When completely blended, turn into 10-inch skillet (or 8-inch square pan) and bake 35 minutes in a 350° oven.

SUNSHINE CAKE

(10-inch cake)

1 cup sifted flour	*7 egg whites*
1¼ cups sugar	*⅓ teaspoon cream of*
5 egg yolks	*tartar*
⅛ teaspoon salt	*2 teaspoons vanilla*

Measure flour and set aside. Measure sugar and also set aside. Beat egg yolks until thick and lemon-colored. Add salt to unbeaten egg whites. With clean, dry beater, whip whites to a foam, then add cream of tartar to them. Continue beating until very stiff.

Add sugar, a little bit at a time, to egg whites, beating in each addition. Beat in yolks and flavoring. Lightly fold in flour, one spoonful at a time.

Turn into ungreased 10-inch tube pan. Bake 35 minutes at 350°.

SUGAR CAKE

(3 8-inch round cakes)

Sugar Cakes are in a category all by themselves. Some visiting folks "from away off" call them our coffeecakes, but they are more than that. They are just right for our "three o'clock piece" in the afternoon.

1¾ cups sugar
½ cup lard
3 eggs, beaten
3 cups flour, unsifted
1 teaspoon baking soda

1 teaspoon cream of
tartar
1 cup buttermilk
3 tablespoons sugar

Mix the sugar and lard, creaming thoroughly until light. Stir in the beaten eggs. Add the next 3 ingredients alternately with the buttermilk.

Pour into 3 8-inch greased pans. Sprinkle 1 tablespoon sugar over the top of each. Bake 25 minutes in a 350° oven. Cut in wedges to serve.

APEAS CAKE

(1 9-inch cake)

Also called *Epee Kuche*. The name is often confused with A.P.'s Cookies.* However, this is the breakfast cake of Berks County, where it is as popular as Shoo-Fly Pie,* and that is very popular! Most cooks bake from four to seven at a time, sizes ranging from five to nine inches in diameter and as high as four inches. This recipe has been cut down proportionally.

2 cups flour, unsifted
1 cup light brown sugar
½ teaspoon baking
  powder
½ cup lard
1 egg

¾ cup milk
½ teaspoon baking soda
1 tablespoon vinegar
1 tablespoon cinnamon
  sugar

Place in a large bowl the flour, sugar, baking powder. Cut in the shortening until the particles are the size of peas. Beat the egg, combine with milk, then add to dry ingredients. Beat until smooth. Stir in baking soda that has been dissolved in vinegar.

Put into a 9-inch piepan that has been greased. Sprinkle the cinnamon sugar over the top. Bake in a 350° oven for 30 to 35 minutes.

BREAKFAST CAKE

(2 9-inch crumb cakes)

1 pound light brown sugar	*½ teaspoon nutmeg*
2 cups flour, unsifted	*1 teaspoon baking soda*
½ cup lard	*1 cup buttermilk*
½ teaspoon salt	*1 egg, well beaten*

Rub the first 5 ingredients together to form crumbs. Reserve ½ cup of the crumbs. To the rest, add the soda, dissolved in buttermilk, and the beaten egg. Beat only until all crumbs are moistened.

Put into 2 9-inch greased piepans. Sprinkle reserved crumbs on the top. Bake in hot oven, 425°, for 25 minutes.

CRUMB CAKE I

(2 9-inch cakes)

Cinnamon is the only spice in this one.

2 cups brown sugar	*1½ cups buttermilk*
½ cup lard	*1 cup brown sugar*
1 egg, beaten	*¾ cup flour*
2½ cups flour	*2 tablespoons butter*
1 teaspoon cinnamon	*1 teaspoon cinnamon*
1 teaspoon baking soda	

Cream sugar and lard together until fluffy. Add egg and stir until creamy. Sift together the flour and cinnamon. Dissolve soda in buttermilk. Add flour to creamed mixture alternately with buttermilk. Mix thoroughly after each addition. Pour immediately into 2 9-inch cake pans that have been greased.

With hands, work together the brown sugar, flour, butter, and cinnamon to make crumbs. Spread on top of cakes. Bake in a moderate oven, 375°, for 35 to 40 minutes.

CRUMB CAKE II

(6×10-inch coffeecake)

A good cake—easy to make because crumbs on top are part of cake mixture.

1½ cups sifted flour
2 teaspoons baking
powder
¼ pound butter
1 cup sugar

1 teaspoon nutmeg
(optional)
2 eggs
½ cup milk

Combine the flour, baking powder, butter, and sugar in a large bowl. (Cut in butter as for pastry.) Reserve 1½ cups crumbs for the top. Add to remaining mixture the nutmeg, eggs, and milk and beat until mixed. Batter will be thin.

Pour into 6×10-inch pan that has been well greased. Top with crumbs. Bake in a 350° oven for 30 minutes. Serve hot or cold.

CREAM CAKE

(1 9×13-inch cake)

2 cups sugar
3 eggs, beaten
2 cups sifted flour
2 teaspoons baking
  powder

½ teaspoon salt
1 cup coffee cream

Cream sugar and eggs together until light. Add the flour, baking powder, and salt that have been sifted together, alternately with the cream.

Bake in a greased 9×13-inch cake pan for about 40 minutes at 350°.

MRS. EMAN'S CRUMB CAKE

(2 8-inch rounds)

An all-purpose cake with a delicious flavor. It is used as a breakfast cake or as a dessert.

3 cups sifted flour
2 cups sugar
½ teaspoon cloves
½ teaspoon allspice

1 cup lard
1 teaspoon baking soda
1 cup milk

Mix together the flour, sugar, spices, and lard until crumbly. Reserve 1 cup of these crumbs for topping. Dissolve soda in milk. Add milk to mixture, stirring until blended. Pour batter into 2 greased and floured 8-inch piepans. Top with crumbs. Bake 35 minutes at 350°.

BLOTCH KUCHA (Drop Cake)

(A 9×12-inch sheet cake)

This one is also known as Sugar Leb Cake (Honey Cake). Not all cooks put nuts on the top to make it fancy. Some just make it plain!

2 cups light brown sugar	1 teaspoon baking
¼ cup butter	powder
¼ cup lard	½ teaspoon baking soda
1 egg, beaten	1 egg, slightly beaten
1 cup buttermilk	½ cup broken walnuts
3 cups flour	

Cream together the sugar and shortenings. Add the beaten egg and buttermilk and blend together. Sift together the flour, baking powder, and baking soda, and mix with creamed ingredients. *Blotch* (drop) on a greased and floured cookie sheet and spread evenly with the back of a spoon.

Brush top with slightly beaten egg. Sprinkle with nuts. Bake in 350° oven "until it springs back when touched with finger."

APPLESAUCE CAKE

(9×13-inch loaf)

1 cup vegetable	½ teaspoon cloves
shortening	½ teaspoon nutmeg
1 cup sugar	1 cup English walnuts,
2 cups applesauce	chopped
1 15-ounce box raisins	2 teaspoons baking soda
2 cups flour	¼ cup hot water
2 teaspoons cinnamon	

Cream together the shortening and sugar. Add applesauce and raisins and mix well. Sift together the flour and spices and add. Beat until thoroughly mixed. Fold in nuts. Lastly, add the baking soda dissolved in hot water. Bake in greased and floured 9×13-inch pan for an hour at 350°.

BLACK JOE CHOCOLATE CAKE

(2 8-inch layers)

Judging from the requests for this recipe, grandmothers all over Dutch Country must have baked Black Joe Chocolate Cakes.

2 cups brown sugar
½ cup shortening (scant)
2 eggs, beaten
½ cup buttermilk
2 cups sifted flour

4 tablespoons cocoa
1 teaspoon vanilla
1 teaspoon baking soda
½ cup boiling water

Cream the sugar and shortening together thoroughly. Blend in the 2 beaten eggs. To this add the buttermilk alternately with the flour and cocoa. Stir in the vanilla. Lastly, add the baking soda dissolved in the boiling water.

Bake in 2 greased and floured 8-inch layer pans for 35 minutes at 350°.

DARK CHOCOLATE CAKE

(2 8-inch layers)

In Pennsylvania, particularly in the Dutch section, practically everybody's favorite cake is a chocolate cake. The darker it is, the better. In one of the cookbooks put out by a local church, sixteen out of sixty-five cake recipes are for chocolate cakes. Could it be a coincidence that three big chocolate manufacturers are located in the Pennsylvania Dutch area?

2 cups light brown sugar	1 teaspoon cream of
¼ cup butter	tartar
¼ cup lard	1 teaspoon baking soda
2 eggs, well beaten	½ cup sour cream
½ cup cocoa	½ cup boiling water
2 cups sifted flour	

Cream together thoroughly the sugar, butter, and lard. Stir in the well-beaten eggs and cocoa. Sift together the flour, cream of tartar, and soda. Add alternately with sour cream to cocoa mixture. Lastly, stir in the boiling water.

Pour into 2 greased 8-inch cake pans. Bake for 35 minutes at 325°. May I suggest Caramel Icing*?

ICE CREAM CAKE

(2 8-inch layers)

A wedding cake recipe! Aunt Ellen used to bake wedding cakes—the kind that melted in your mouth. All kinds of pans were used to get the proper size layers. I remember being inquisitive about the pan she used for the bottom layer. It was a large dishpan!

2 cups sugar	1 cup milk
¾ cup butter	1 teaspoon almond or
2 cups sifted flour	vanilla flavoring
3 teaspoons baking	5 stiffly beaten egg
powder	whites
1 cup cornstarch	

Cream the sugar and butter together. Sift the flour, baking powder, and cornstarch together. Add these alternately with milk to creamed mixture. Beat until very smooth. Add vanilla and then fold in egg whites that have been beaten until stiff.

Bake in 2 greased and floured 8-inch layer pans for 25 to 30 minutes in a 350° oven.

BLACK WALNUT CAKE

(2 8-inch layers or 1 9×13-inch loaf)

This is my absolute favorite!

½ cup butter
1½ cups sugar
1 teaspoon baking
    powder
2 cups flour

¾ cup cold water
1 cup black walnuts,
    chopped
4 egg whites

Cream butter and gradually add the sugar, creaming until light and fluffy. Sift together the baking powder and flour. Add it alternately with the water to the creamed mixture. Fold in the chopped walnuts. Beat the egg whites until stiff but not dry. Carefully fold them into the batter.

Bake in 2 8-inch layer cake pans for 30 to 35 minutes in a 350° oven. Frost with Boiled White Icing* and black walnuts.

LEMON COCONUT CAKE

(4 8-inch layers, or 2 8-inch layers and 20 cupcakes)

Adapted from an old, old recipe that called for pearl ash as a leavening agent. A delicious cake that stays fresh for days.

½ pound butter
3 cups sugar
5 eggs
grated rind and juice of
  1 lemon

1 cup buttermilk
3 teaspoons baking
  powder
4 cups sifted flour

Cream together the butter and sugar. Add eggs, one at a time, beating until light after each addition. Add the lemon rind and juice to the buttermilk. Sift the baking powder with the flour that has been previously sifted and measured. Add to creamed mixture alternately with the buttermilk. Beat until smooth.

Pour into greased layer cake pans. Bake in a 350° oven for 30 minutes (20 minutes for cupcakes). Frost with Fluffy Confectioners' Icing* and coconut.

OLD-FASHIONED SPICECAKE

(9×13-inch loaf)

2 cups sugar
½ cup butter and lard,
  mixed
3 eggs, beaten
2½ cups flour
1½ teaspoons cocoa

½ teaspoon cloves
½ teaspoon allspice
1 teaspoon cinnamon
1½ teaspoons baking
  soda
1 cup buttermilk

Cream together the sugar, butter, and lard. Add eggs and beat until light. Sift together all dry ingredients and add alternately with buttermilk. Beat for 2 minutes.

Pour into 9×13-inch loaf pan that has been greased and floured. Bake at 350° for 40 to 45 minutes. Cover with your favorite white icing.

MORNING GLORY CAKE

(A cornucopia of 48 cones)

A cake that takes four or five hours to make! Years ago I was told about the old-time Morning Glory Cake. When I finally saw one, it was called a Tulip Cake. Others since have told me of other names: Toota Cake, Band Cake, Ice Cream Cone Cake, Easter Lily Cake, Bride's Cake, Cornucopia Cake, and Funnel Cake.

Fifty years ago, this cake was often decorated in red, white, and blue for Memorial Day celebrations and Fourth of July picnics. Some called it Band Cake because it was a popular donation item for the annual band festival. Even more decorative was the Ice Cream Cone Cake that had a cherry in each cone and a floral decoration of real flowers inserted in the top.

Not very many cooks today take the time nor have the patience to make Morning Glory Cakes. However, some are baked for birthdays, bridal showers, and weddings. Wedding cakes are iced in white, but for other occasions the cake icing usually matches table decorations. Quite often it is used as a table centerpiece.

The Morning Glory Cake is made with a spongecake batter. It is a unique cake to serve. Each guest lifts out his own cone, and the cake isn't even cut!

9 eggs	1 teaspoon vanilla
2 cups sugar	2 tablespoons water
2 tablespoons water	1 cup confectioners'
2 cups sifted flour	sugar
2 teaspoons baking	colored sugar
powder	

Heat oven to 350°.

Beat the eggs with a wire whisk until frothy. Adding the sugar very slowly, one tablespoon at a time, continue beating for 15 minutes. Add water and beat until blended. Gradually fold in the flour and baking powder that have been sifted together. Add vanilla. While the first cones are baking, make icing by mixing water and confectioners' sugar until smooth.

For baking the cones of a Morning Glory Cake, one should have at least 3 aluminum piepans, 9-inch size. Using each pan 4 times (4 cones from each cake), you will have 48 cones. With a large mixing spoon put 3 spoonfuls of batter in each ungreased pan, or just enough to cover the bottom. Bake for 8 minutes at 350°.

When baked, cut into 4 wedges and roll each piece into a cone, working quickly while cake is warm. Dip open end of each cone in icing and then in colored sugar. Arrange circle of cones on cake plate so that the diameter of first layer is 9 inches, with points of cones toward the center. Repeat for other layers, making the circumference of each layer smaller than the last. Use halves of broken or crippled cones to fill hollow spots in the center.

LOLLY'S CAKE

(A 3-layer 8-inch cake)

A delicious cake with an unusual filling and icing.

1 cup sugar
½ cup lard or ⅔ cup vegetable shortening
3 eggs
¼ cup baking molasses, mild-flavored
2 cups sifted flour

1 teaspoon baking soda
1 tablespoon cinnamon
⅛ teaspoon salt
¾ cup buttermilk
Lolly's Cake Filling and Icing*

Cream together the sugar and lard. Blend in the eggs, one at a time. Beat until smooth. Add molasses and mix well. Sift together dry ingredients and add alternately with buttermilk. Put into 3 greased 8-inch round cake pans. If you have only 2 8-inch layer cake pans, use an 8-inch piepan to invert for top layer. Bake in a moderate oven, 350°, for 20 minutes. Complete with Lolly's Cake Filling and Icing.*

LOLLY'S CAKE FILLING AND ICING

(For an 8-inch 2-layer cake)

2 beaten egg yolks	2 tablespoons butter
¾ cup sugar	1 cup raisins
1 tablespoon flour	1 teaspoon vanilla
1 cup milk	

In a saucepan mix together the egg yolks, sugar, and flour. Gradually stir in the milk. Add butter and raisins. Bring to a boil and boil for just 1 full minute, stirring constantly. Remove from heat and add vanilla. Cool and spread between layers and over top of cake, letting a bit run down over sides.

CARAMEL ICING

(For an 8-inch 2-layer cake)

1 cup brown sugar	½ cup buttermilk
½ cup white sugar	1 tablespoon butter

Cook the brown and white sugar with the buttermilk until it forms a soft ball in water (238°). Cool to lukewarm, then add the tablespoon of butter. Beat until creamy. If icing seems too stiff, add a tablespoon of milk or cream.

BOILED WHITE ICING

(Enough for top and sides of 8-inch 2-layer cake)

2 cups sugar
⅔ cup boiling water
⅛ teaspoon cream of
tartar

2 egg whites, stiffly
beaten
1 teaspoon vanilla

In a saucepan combine sugar, boiling water, and cream of tartar, stirring until sugar is dissolved. Boil without stirring until syrup *begins* to spin a thread (235°). At this point, take out 3 tablespoons of the sugar mixture, adding one at a time to the egg whites.

Cook syrup until it is really spinning a thread (240°). Add all of syrup very slowly to egg whites, beating until the desired consistency is reached. Stir in vanilla flavoring.

FLUFFY CONFECTIONERS' ICING

(For top and sides of 2-layer cake)

2 egg whites
2 tablespoons water
⅛ teaspoon salt
⅛ teaspoon cream of
tartar

3½ cups confectioners'
sugar
1 teaspoon vanilla or
grated lemon rind

Beat together the egg whites and water until stiff. Add salt and cream of tartar and beat in. Slowly add confectioners' sugar, beating all the while. Add flavoring.

FUDGE FROSTING

(Enough for a 2-layer cake)

2 *squares baking*	1½ *cups sugar*
chocolate	2 *tablespoons butter*
½ *cup milk or cream*	1 *teaspoon vanilla*

In a quart-size saucepan melt the chocolate over very low heat. Add milk or cream and sugar. Boil slowly until it forms a soft ball (238°). Add butter and vanilla. Remove from heat.

Let stand undisturbed a few minutes. Beat until cool enough to spread. If frosting gets too thick, add a tablespoon of cream.

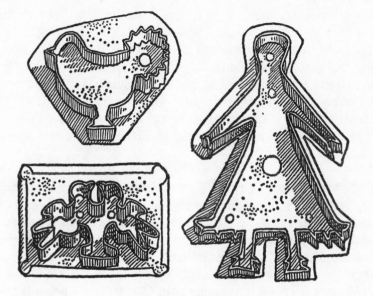

Cookies

MUCH has been written about Christmas among the
Pennsylvania Dutch—in particular, the Moravians—and all
writers have acknowledged that cookies have an important part
in this celebration. Ruth Hutchison says, in *The Pennsylvania
Dutch Cookbook,* "There used to be a saying in Bethlehem that
you could estimate not only the family's culinary skill but its
financial status from the quantity and variety of its Christmas
cookies." Originality in cookie baking and decorating knows no
limits in Bethlehem, Pennsylvania. The most unique I have seen
is the string of fish: cookie fishes given by one family to each
child after he has heard the Christmas story beside the "Putz."
'Tis a forceful reminder that the Christ of Christmas wants each

of His children to be "fishers of men!" In this particular home, each December, hundreds of cookie fishes are baked and strung together right through the eyes—five fishes on a string.

Among cutout cookies, animal cookies predominate in number, but there are also men, women, and children, Indians, Pilgrims, and other historical figures. One family has collected over six hundred antique cookie cutters with not one duplicate! With these cutters the Moravians make cookies from either light or dark dough, known today as white Moravian cookies and Brown Moravian Cookies.*

Sandtarts* are the pride and joy of the Pennsylvania Dutch Christmas baking. They are the most time-consuming too. They are rolled very thin (sisters and cousins vie for the honor of having the thinnest) and then brushed with egg white, covered with finely chopped pecans or peanuts, and sprinkled with cinnamon. That is a four-step finishing process for decoration, but they are well worth the effort.

Cookies baked at times other than Christmas are much larger —so large that they are commonly called cakes. For the most part, they are at least three inches in diameter and as thick as a gingerbread man. In a region where cooks bake everything large —pies, dumplings, and loaves of bread—it seems altogether natural that the cookies should be large. The two most popular of these are the Soft Sugar Cakes* and the Molasses Cakes that are glazed with an egg yolk, brushed on before baking.

In cookie baking, molasses is the most popular flavoring, but spices, coconut, honey, chocolate, and fruit (raisins, dates, and currants) abound also. Lemon flavoring and almond flavoring are commonly used, and in a few homes sherry is added to the common sugar cookies. As for Grandmother's rose-water flavoring, the desire for that is now as rare as the pearl ash and hartshorn that she used to use for leavening. Anise and caraway appear more often. Hickory nuts may be hard to find, but peanuts, almonds, black walnuts, and English walnuts are used for decoration and flavoring.

One sugar cookie has caused much ado among historians.

They cannot agree on the name or the origin. It has been called A.P.'s,* Apees, Apiece, Apace, Apise, and Apeas. One story identifies it with the cookie that Ann Page sold from her basket on the streets of Philadelphia around 1830. Having quite an eye for business, she imprinted her initials on the cookies. The controversy over A.P. cakes really becomes entangled when the coffeecake made in the Oley Valley and called *Epee Kuche* is suggested as the A.P. cake. The Apees-Apiece-Apeas fuss may be solved one of these years, but the story of Pennsylvania Dutch cookies—white, brown, plain, or fancy—will live on.

SANDTARTS

(14 dozen)

The most delicious of all Christmas cookies, yet made only for Christmas. A thin, crisp cookie with cinnamon sugar and chopped nuts on top. The nuts are either peanuts, pecans, or almonds.

2 cups sugar
½ pound butter
2 eggs, beaten
4 cups sifted flour

2 slightly beaten egg
whites
cinnamon or cinnamon
sugar
1 cup chopped nuts

Cream together the sugar and butter. Stir in the beaten eggs. Add flour and mix thoroughly. Chill overnight.

Roll out on floured board to ⅛-inch thickness or as thin as possible. Cut into rounds, squares, or rectangles and lift onto cookie sheet. Before baking, brush egg whites over the top, sprinkle with cinnamon or cinnamon sugar, then top with nuts. Bake from 8 to 10 minutes in a 350° oven.

WHITE CHRISTMAS COOKIES

(12 dozen)

2 cups sugar
1 cup butter
3 eggs, beaten
5 cups flour
1 teaspoon baking soda

½ teaspoon cinnamon
2 tablespoons milk
nuts, whole or broken
    kernels, as desired

Cream together the sugar and butter. Add the beaten eggs and blend thoroughly. Sift together the flour, soda, and cinnamon. Stir these into the creamed mixture. Moisten with milk. Chill dough overnight.

Roll out dough on floured board to ⅛-inch thickness. Cut out with cookie cutters. Before baking, press nuts into tops of cookies. Bake until lightly browned in a 350° oven.

A.P.'S COOKIES

(10 dozen 3-inch cookies)

This sugar cookie has much folklore connected with it. Did Ann Page cut her initials on the cookies she sold on the streets of Philadelphia? This is supposed to be the recipe for the cookies she sold. Who knows? Maybe it is and maybe it isn't.

2 cups sugar
1 cup butter
5 eggs, well beaten
½ cup cream

1 teaspoon vanilla
1 teaspoon baking soda
4½ cups flour, unsifted

Cream together the sugar and butter. Add the well-beaten eggs, cream, and vanilla. Mix thoroughly. Add the baking soda and flour, sifted together. Mix until all ingredients are completely blended. Chill overnight.

On a lightly floured board, roll out small portions of dough as thin as possible. Cut with round 3-inch cookie cutter. Mark an *A.P.* on each round if you like. Bake at 350° until slightly browned.

WALNUT WAFERS

(5 dozen dainty cookies)

2 eggs
1 cup plus 2 tablespoons
   brown sugar
4 tablespoons flour

¼ teaspoon baking
   powder
⅓ teaspoon salt
½ pound black walnut
   kernels

Beat the eggs and add to them the brown sugar, flour, baking powder, and salt that have been sifted together. Mix thoroughly. Fold in the nuts. Drop from a teaspoon onto a greased cookie sheet.

Bake 7 minutes in a 325° oven. Let stand on cookie sheet 90 seconds before removing.

BROWN MORAVIAN COOKIES

(5 dozen cookies)

½ cup lard
½ cup butter
1 cup light brown sugar
1 cup New Orleans
   mild-flavored baking
   molasses (as Gold
   Label Brer Rabbit)

4 cups sifted flour
1 teaspoon ginger
1 tablespoon cinnamon
¼ teaspoon cloves
¼ teaspoon nutmeg
1 teaspoon baking soda
¼ cup warm water

Cream together the shortening and sugar. Stir in the molasses. Add the flour which has been resifted with the spices. Mix thoroughly. Lastly, stir in the soda which has been dissolved in warm water. When blended, cover and chill overnight.

On a floured board roll out very thin. Cut out cookies with cutters of birds, animals, men, and stars. Bake in a 325° oven for 10 to 12 minutes.

MRS. DECKERT'S TEA COOKIES

(12 dozen cutout cookies)

1 cup granulated sugar
1 cup light brown sugar
½ cup butter
3 eggs, beaten
2 teaspoons vanilla
flavoring
1 teaspoon baking soda
2 tablespoons boiling
water

4 cups flour
1 teaspoon baking
powder
1 egg, beaten
¼ cup cinnamon sugar
¼ cup chopped nuts

Cream together granulated sugar, brown sugar, and butter. Blend in the 3 beaten eggs and vanilla. Dissolve soda in boiling water and add to creamed mixture. Sift flour and baking powder together into mixture. Mix thoroughly. Cover and chill overnight in refrigerator.

When rolling out on floured board, roll about ⅛ of the dough at a time, keeping remainder of dough in refrigerator. Roll very thin. Cut out with floured cutters and lift with spatula onto cookie sheet.

Using pastry brush, spread each cookie with beaten egg. Sprinkle with cinnamon sugar and chopped nuts. (Or, they can be baked without any topping, then iced later.) Bake 6 to 8 minutes in 375° oven.

COCONUT SUGAR COOKIES

(10 dozen 2-inch cookies)

Another large-yield recipe suited for Christmas baking.

1 cup sour cream
1 teaspoon baking soda
1 teaspoon cream of
  tartar
3 eggs
2 cups sugar
2 teaspoons vanilla

½ cup butter
½ cup vegetable
  shortening
1 cup coconut
3¾ cups flour, unsifted
¼ cup coconut

Put sour cream into a medium bowl. Stir into it the baking soda and cream of tartar.

In a large bowl beat together the eggs, sugar, and vanilla. Add butter and vegetable shortening. Beat until well mixed. Add sour cream and mix again. Stir in the 1 cup coconut. Fold in the flour until completely mixed. Drop from a teaspoon onto cookie sheet. Use ¼ cup coconut to garnish tops of cookies. Bake for 6 minutes in 450° oven.

OATMEAL CRISPIES

(7 dozen 2-inch cookies)

¾ cup lard or vegetable
  shortening
1 cup dark brown sugar
½ cup granulated sugar
2 eggs, beaten
1 teaspoon vanilla

1½ cups sifted flour
1 teaspoon salt
1 teaspoon baking soda
3 cups quick-cooking
  oatmeal
½ cup chopped nuts

Cream lard with both kinds of sugar. Add beaten eggs and vanilla. Sift together flour, salt, and soda. Stir into creamed mixture. Add oatmeal and nuts. Blend thoroughly.

Drop from a teaspoon onto cookie sheets and bake from 8 to 10 minutes at 350°.

SALEM CAKES

(8 dozen)

½ cup butter	3 cups sifted flour
2 cups brown sugar	2 teaspoons nutmeg
2 eggs, well beaten	1 teaspoon baking soda

Cream butter and brown sugar together until very creamy. Stir in the well-beaten eggs. Measure flour and resift with nutmeg and soda. Combine both mixtures thoroughly. Chill for 3 hours or more.

Roll out to ¼-inch thickness. Cut in desired shapes. Bake 8 minutes at 350°.

FILLED COOKIES

(3 dozen)

1 cup shortening	3 teaspoons baking
1 cup sugar	powder
1 egg, beaten	¼ teaspoon salt
½ cup milk	1 teaspoon vanilla
4 cups sifted flour	

Cream the shortening and sugar together. Add the beaten egg and milk. Into this creamed mixture sift the flour, baking powder, and salt. Add the vanilla and mix well. Chill for several hours.

Roll out on floured board until thin, and cut with round cookie cutter. Drop a teaspoon of the following filling on half of the rounds. Top with another cookie. Then, with a fork, press the two together firmly around edges.

Bake in 350° oven for about 15 minutes.

COOKIE FILLING:

1½ cups raisins, chopped	½ cup sugar
8 dates, chopped	1 teaspoon flour
¾ cup water	

Mix the above and cook until thick, stirring all the while to prevent burning. Cool before putting on cookies.

BUTTERSCOTCH COOKIES

(6½ dozen cookies)

An all-year-round cookie! Very good flavor and keeps well.

½ cup butter	1 teaspoon baking soda
½ cup lard	1 teaspoon baking
2 cups brown sugar	powder
3 eggs, beaten	½ teaspoon salt
2 teaspoons vanilla	½ cup nuts, broken
3 cups flour	

Cream together the butter, lard, and brown sugar. Add the beaten eggs and vanilla. Sift together the flour, soda, baking powder, and salt. Combine with creamed mixture and blend thoroughly. Stir in the nuts.

Drop from a teaspoon onto cookie sheets. Bake 10 minutes at 350°.

MOLASSES DROP COOKIES

(8 dozen 2-inch cookies)

A good combination of spice, molasses, nuts, and raisins.

1 cup vegetable shortening	4 cups sifted flour
½ cup brown sugar	2 teaspoons baking soda
½ cup dark table syrup (Karo)	1 teaspoon cinnamon
½ cup baking molasses (mild-flavored)	¼ teaspoon ginger
1 cup buttermilk	½ teaspoon salt
	1 cup seedless raisins
	1 cup chopped walnuts

Preheat oven to 375°.

Cream together the shortening and sugar. Blend in the syrup and molasses and then the buttermilk.

Sift together the flour, soda, spices, and salt, sifting right into the first mixture. Toss in the raisins and nuts so they get coated with flour before stirring. Mix together thoroughly. Drop by teaspoonfuls onto cookie sheets and bake 8 to 10 minutes.

CHOCOLATE JUMBLES

(8 dozen 3-inch cookies)

1 cup butter	3 teaspoons baking powder
2 cups sugar	½ teaspoon salt
4 eggs, well beaten	3 cups confectioners' sugar
8 ounces baking chocolate	6 tablespoons cream
3 cups flour, unsifted	1 teaspoon vanilla

Cream the butter and sugar thoroughly. Add the well-beaten eggs. Melt the chocolate over hot water. Add the chocolate to the creamed mixture. Sift together the flour, baking powder, and salt and combine with the chocolate mixture. Chill overnight.

Roll out very thin on floured board and cut with round 3-inch cutter. Bake for 7 minutes in a 350° oven. When cool, spread with the following icing: combine the confectioners' sugar, cream, and vanilla. Beat until smooth.

LEBKUCHEN

(10 dozen)

In the Pennsylvania Dutch dialect *leb* means honey. So this is a honey cake without the honey.

2 cups sugar	1 teaspoon ground
1¼ cups lard	nutmeg
2 eggs	2 teaspoons cinnamon
1 quart molasses, not	1 teaspoon cinnamon or
baking molasses	coriander
¼ pound citron, cut fine	1½ cups buttermilk
12 cups flour	1¼ cups chopped nuts,
2 tablespoons baking	pecans or walnuts
soda	3 cups 10X
2 teaspoons anise seed	confectioners' sugar
1 teaspoon ground cloves	⅓ cup water

Cream together the sugar and lard. Beat the eggs and stir into creamed mixture. Add molasses and citron and mix well. Sift together the flour, baking soda, and spices, and add alternately with buttermilk to first mixture. Mix in the nuts, then cover and refrigerate overnight.

On lightly floured board, roll dough to ¼-inch thickness. Cut

into 2×3-inch rectangles. Bake in a 375° oven for 10 minutes.
When cool, spread with icing made by combining the confectioners' sugar and water. It will be a very thin icing but will harden.

FRUIT AND NUT DROPS

(6 dozen 2-inch cookies)

½ cup butter	1 teaspoon baking soda
1½ cups brown sugar	2 tablespoons warm
2 eggs, beaten	water
⅓ cup milk	1 cup walnuts, chopped
2 cups flour	1 cup raisins

Cream together butter and brown sugar. Blend in 2 beaten eggs and ⅓ cup milk. Add the flour. Dissolve soda in warm water and add to mixture. Mix thoroughly. Stir in walnuts and raisins. Drop from teaspoon onto cookie sheets. Bake 8 minutes at 375°.

CHOCOLATE NUT DROP COOKIES

(5 dozen)

½ cup shortening	2 teaspoons baking
1 cup sugar	powder
1 egg yolk	½ cup milk
2 squares baking	1 cup chopped nuts
chocolate	1 teaspoon vanilla
1½ cups flour	

Cream together the shortening and sugar. Add egg yolk and beat. Melt the chocolate over low heat and add. Sift together the flour and baking powder and add alternately with milk. Stir in chopped nuts and vanilla. Drop from teaspoon and bake at 375° about 8 minutes.

HONEY CAKES

(1½ dozen large cookies)

Too big to call a cookie; the Pennsylvania Dutch call them cakes.

1 cup honey
2 tablespoons butter
½ cup light brown sugar
2½ cups sifted flour
1 teaspoon baking
powder

½ teaspoon baking soda
½ teaspoon salt
1 egg yolk, beaten
¼ cup buttermilk

Heat the honey to boiling. Add to it the butter and light brown sugar, stirring until sugar is dissolved. Cool 10 minutes. Meanwhile, measure flour and sift with baking powder, baking soda, and salt. Add the honey mixture to the beaten egg yolk and then to sifted dry ingredients. Add the buttermilk and mix well. Chill overnight.

Roll on floured board to ⅓-inch thickness. Cut out with 3-inch round cutter. Bake 12 minutes at 350°.

SPICE TONGUES

(6 dozen)

A flavorful large cookie that keeps well.

1 cup brown sugar
1 cup lard
2 cups mild-flavored
  baking molasses
5½ cups flour
1 teaspoon ginger

1 tablespoon cinnamon
1 tablespoon baking
  soda
½ cup warm water
granulated sugar

Cream together the sugar and lard. Blend in the molasses. Measure the flour before sifting, then sift together with spices and soda. Add alternately with water to the first mixture. Chill overnight.

To shape next day: make balls of dough 1 inch in diameter. In the palm of your hand, flatten into the shape of a tongue. Place on cookie sheet 2 inches apart. Sprinkle with granulated sugar. Bake for 12 minutes at 350°.

SOFT SUGAR CAKES

(4 dozen)

A good cookie for dunking.

2 cups sugar
1 cup shortening
  (butter and lard)
1 cup sour cream
4 eggs
1 teaspoon baking soda

1 teaspoon cream of
  tartar
6 cups sifted flour
granulated sugar
¼ cup cooked raisins,
  (optional)

Thoroughly cream the sugar and shortening together. Stir in the sour cream and eggs. Resift flour with baking soda and cream of tartar. Add to creamed mixture. Mix well. Chill overnight.

Roll on floured board to ¼-inch thickness. Cut out with 3-inch round cookie cutter. Sprinkle sugar on the tops. If you like, decorate with cooked raisins in the center. Bake for 8 to 10 minutes at 400°.

MOLASSES CAKES

(4 dozen)

These are the thick, soft molasses cookies, excellent for dunking. The top coating, effected with egg yolks, is quite shiny.

*2 cups light brown
sugar
1½ cups lard
1¾ cups New Orleans
molasses
5 teaspoons baking
soda*

*2 cups buttermilk
6 cups flour, unsifted
½ teaspoon salt
2 egg yolks, beaten*

Cream the sugar and lard thoroughly, then add the molasses and blend. Mix the soda with the buttermilk and add to the sugar mixture alternately with the flour and salt. Store in a covered bowl overnight in the refrigerator.

In the morning, drop batter from a tablespoon onto a cookie sheet about 2 inches apart. Flatten slightly and brush with beaten egg yolks. Bake for 10 minutes at 375°.

Candy

ALTHOUGH plenty of fudge, peanut brittle, and opera creams are made by our cooks today, it is only the very old candy recipes that are presented in this chapter. Potato Candy,* Moravian Mints,* and Molasses Mosies* are made any time throughout the winter, while coconut candies are special treats for Christmas and Easter.

The Peach Leather* and Apple Leather* are not really candies, but might be called candy substitutes. The men who go deer hunting claim that this delicacy is the hunter's delight for munching because it also serves as a thirst quencher.

BOILED CREAM CANDY

(1 pound)

2 cups sugar   *½ teaspoon flavoring*
¾ cup water   *walnut kernels*

Combine the sugar and water, stirring until the sugar is dissolved. Boil without stirring until it sticks together when dropped from a teaspoon into ½ cup of cold water. Remove from heat and beat until creamy. Add flavoring and beat until thoroughly blended. Shape into balls, about ½ inch in diameter. Place on a plate and press a walnut kernel into the top.

MORAVIAN MINTS

(1 pound)

1 pound 10X sugar
4 tablespoons water
7 drops oil of peppermint or spearmint

Put 10X sugar in top of double boiler over boiling water. Add the 4 tablespoons of water and allow to dissolve. Add the flavoring. When the mixture hardens slightly on top, it is ready to drop on wax paper. Mints should be only an inch in diameter.

MOLASSES MOSIES

(1½ pounds)

2 cups molasses   *½ cup walnut kernels,*
1 cup granulated sugar   *coarsely broken*
1 tablespoon vinegar   *(optional)*
1 tablespoon butter

Put all ingredients except nuts into a large skillet. Boil slowly until candy thermometer reaches 310°, or until a little of the mixture dripping into cold water makes a hard thread. Butter tiny muffin pans or mosie pans and cover with a layer of chopped nuts. Fill ⅓ full of candy mixture. Cool in refrigerator.

Note: This candy can also be made in buttered cake pans or piepans and then broken when hard.

POTATO CANDY

(1 pound)

1 small potato	*1 pound 10X sugar*
dash of salt	*1 teaspoon vanilla*
1 tablespoon butter	*⅓ cup peanut butter*

Peel potato and quarter. Cook in water until soft. Drain. In a bowl mash potato with salt and butter. Add sugar, one third at a time, beating until smooth and well blended. Mix in the vanilla. If mixture is not stiff enough to roll, add more sugar.

Roll out between 2 sheets of wax paper until it is ⅛ inch thick. Spread with the peanut butter. Roll up like a jelly roll. Chill for an hour, then slice into ¼-inch pieces. Let ripen a day.

COCONUT CREAM EASTER EGGS

(2 pounds)

1 medium-size potato	*3 pounds confectioners'*
1 coconut	*sugar*
¼ teaspoon salt	*1 pound dipping*
1 teaspoon vanilla	*chocolate*

Peel and cook the potato in salted water until soft. Meanwhile, peel the coconut and grate or put through food chopper. Drain liquid from cooked potato amd mash. Thoroughly mix the potato, coconut, salt, and vanilla. Gradually add the sugar and mix until thoroughly blended. Let stand overnight to ripen. In the morning, shape into eggs and dip into the chocolate which has been melted over boiling water. Set eggs on wax paper to harden.

PEACH LEATHER

For leisure chewing.

Cover the bottom of buttered piepans with halves of peeled peaches. Pound with a potato masher to flatten each half. Dry in the sun one whole day, or in a 200° oven for 4 to 6 hours. (With the old-fashioned wood and coal stoves, we put these in the oven to dry overnight.)

APPLE LEATHER

Spread ¼ inch of apple butter evenly over the bottom of a buttered piepan, or use halves of apples as for Peach Leather.* Dry in the sun for one day, or in a 200° oven 4 to 6 hours.

Beverages

THE "pause that refreshes" is just as descriptive of Grand-father's nine o'clock harvest refreshment as of the grandchil-dren's Coke time. Among the farmers of Pennsylvania Dutch Country, nine o'clock in the morning was the time for lunch. The children usually carried to the fields some Funnel Cakes* or cookies with the beverage, which was, quite often, some homemade wine. A popular choice among harvesters, however, was the vinegar drink called Essich Schling,* or Vinegar Punch.

The Pennsylvania Dutch make and use their wines so quietly that non-Dutch neighbors are often not aware of the amount that is made in their neighbor's cellar. It is not usually served with meals, but adds a bit of health to each day's living after meals and between times. Quite a few take a little wine for the stomach's sake according to St. Paul's admonition. For others, it is pure delight and enjoyed with moderation.

You will find wines made of strawberries, rhubarb, grapes, potatoes, elderberries, dandelion, currants, cherries, blackberries, apricots, dogwood blossoms, spearmint tea leaves, and white clover. Most wine makers make their wines "by guess," but a friend worked out the recipes in this chapter. One wine maker declared that there are no secrets or tricks to tell, but his wife admonished: "Never, never stir wines on a cloudy day."

There is a certain group of Dutch beverages that can easily be classified as ladies' favorites, since they are the ones served at quilting parties and sewing circles. These are unfermented fruit drinks, teas, and sweet wines.

Grape juice dates back to the earliest years of Pennsylvania history. In fact, our first settlers came from a land of vineyards. For a time, cider became the substitute for the sour wines of the Rhineland, but in a little while sweet wines were made in abundance. These were proudly served until the days of prohibition when wineglasses were gradually pushed to the back of the cupboards. One dear lady carefully wrapped each of her wineglasses and tucked them into the bedroom dresser drawers, "lest someone be offended."

The Pennsylvania Dutch were never great drinkers of imported teas, but they certainly enjoy brewing herb leaves. They use meadow teas of spearmint and peppermint varieties for their hot-weather drinks and dry the same herbs for their winter suppers. During the summer, various punches are made with tea and fruit combinations.

Many fruit syrups are canned for winter use. These include currant, rhubarb, blackberry, raspberry, strawberry, lemon, and cherry syrups. The best of these is Raspberry Shrub.*

ESSICH SCHLING

(Vinegar Punch)

(1 serving)

¼ cup vinegar   dash of nutmeg
¾ cup ice water   (optional)
sugar to taste   ¼ teaspoon baking soda
                           (optional)

Mix all together in a glass and serve immediately.

GINGER WATER

(4 servings)

½ teaspoon ginger
½ cup sugar
1 quart ice water

These amounts can be varied to suit individual taste.

PEACH WINE

1 peck White Hale peaches
11 quarts water
10 pounds sugar

Wash peaches carefully and slice without peeling. Put slices
and peach stones into a large kettle. Add enough of the 11
quarts of water so that peaches are almost covered. Heat to

almost boiling, then remove from heat. Stir in the sugar and the rest of the water. Mix well.

Put into a crock; cover with cheesecloth and let set in a cool cellar for 3 weeks or until fermentation has ceased, stirring twice a week. Strain and bottle but leave unsealed for several days.

VINEGAR GINGER PUNCH

(4 to 5 servings)

1 cup cider vinegar　　　*1 tablespoon ginger*
½ cup molasses　　　　　*1 quart ice water*

Mix together in the order given.

FOX GRAPE WINE

½ bushel fox grapes　　　*4 pounds raisins*
¼ bushel Concord　　　　*35 pounds sugar*
grapes

Heat grapes in water (enough to almost cover) until just about boiling. Put into a crock that contains raisins and sugar. Add 4 quarts of water, cover with a cheesecloth, and let stand in cool cellar about 3 weeks or until fermentation has ceased, stirring twice a week. Strain and bottle but do not seal for 3 days. Lay wine bottles on side to store.

CHERRY WINE

In a 2-gallon crock put 2 quarts sour cherries and 5 pounds sugar. Fill with water. Cover with muslin and tie securely. (Set in sun until Thanksgiving.) Strain and bottle.

GRAPE JUICE

5 pounds grapes
1 quart water
1 pound sugar

Wash grapes, stem, and measure 5 pounds. Add the water, heat, and boil 10 minutes. Strain but do not press. To liquid add sugar and stir until dissolved. Bring to a full boil and bottle.

RASPBERRY SHRUB

(10 servings)

3 pints raspberries   *1 cup lemon juice*
1½ cups sugar   *2 quarts water*
2 cups water

Put the raspberries and sugar in a saucepan with 2 cups water. Boil slowly for 10 minutes. Strain and cool. Add lemon juice with 2 quarts of water. Serve with cracked ice.

RASPBERRY SHRUB SYRUP

Place 2 to 4 quarts of raspberries in a large agateware kettle. Cover with vinegar, but not enough to cause the berries to float. Allow this to stand overnight. In the morning squeeze through a cheesecloth. For each cup of strained liquid, add 1 cup of sugar. Boil for 20 minutes. Bottle, and store in a cool place. To serve, fill glasses ⅓ full and add cold water and ice to dilute.

PEACH BRANDY

A delicious by-product of peach canning.

Fill quart jar with pits and skins of peaches (about 24 peaches needed for enough peelings for 1 quart). Make a medium sugar syrup by dissolving 1 cup sugar in 2 cups water. Pour boiling sugar syrup over peach skins, filling to within 1 inch of top. (Leave this space for freezing expansion.) Seal. Bury 8 inches underground until Christmas. Strain and serve.

Pennsylvania Dutch Menus

Here are suggested menus for breakfasts, dinners, and suppers. You may interchange items if you like.

Breakfast I

STEWED APPLES

OATMEAL

FRIED HAM   FRIED POTATOES WITH EGGS*

SCRAMBLED EGGS

POTATO BUNS*   ELDERBERRY JELLY

SHOO-FLY PIE*

SOFT SUGAR COOKIES*

Breakfast II

SLICED PEACHES
OATMEAL WITH RAISINS
FRIZZLED BEEF IN BROWN MILK GRAVY* ON TOAST
MASHED POTATO CAKES*
CORN MUFFINS*   BLACKBERRY JAM
SCHNITZ PIE*
COCOA   COFFEE

Breakfast III

CANTALOUPE
BRAN CEREAL
SCRAPPLE* AND SAUSAGE   FRIED MUSH*
MOLASSES
HOME-BAKED WHITE BREAD*   APPLE BUTTER*
SCHMIERKASE*
CRUMB CAKES*
GRAPES
MILK   COFFEE

Dinner I

HAM WITH SCHNITZ UN KNEPP*
POTATO FILLING*   DRIED CORN*
CELERY HEARTS   GREEN BEANS
HOMEMADE WHOLE WHEAT BREAD*
APPLE BUTTER*   SCHMIERKASE*
CHOW CHOW*
PICKLED BEETS* AND RED BEET EGGS*
BREAD-AND-BUTTER PICKLES*
CABBAGE SLAW
LOLLY'S CAKE*
COFFEE

Dinner II

BAKED HAM WITH KIMMEL CHERRIES*
FRESH STRING BEANS WITH BROWNED BUTTER
SCALLOPED POTATOES*
CORN PUDDING*
POTATO BUNS*   QUINCE JELLY
PEPPER CABBAGE*
CHOW CHOW*   PICKLED SPICED WATERMELON*
CRISP PICKLE MIX*
APPLESAUCE
FRUITED JELLO
LEMON CAKE PIE*   COFFEE

Dinner III

BOILED CHICKEN POTPIE*
POTATO FILLING*   STEWED ONIONS
SWEET AND SOUR CELERY*
HOMEMADE WHITE BREAD*
SCHMIERKASE*   APPLE BUTTER*
CORN RELISH*   CREAMED CUCUMBERS*
FOURTEEN-DAY SWEET PICKLES*   SPICED SECKEL PEARS*
SNOW PUDDING*
SPICE TONGUE COOKIES*
MORAVIAN MINTS*   COFFEE

Dinner IV

ROAST BEEF
MASHED POTATOES   PEAS
BUTTERED NOODLES   FRIED PUMPKIN*
ENDIVE SALAD WITH BOILED BACON DRESSING*
BREAD AND BUTTER   STRAWBERRY JELLY
MUSTARD BEANS*
SPICED PEACHES*   CORN RELISH*
APPLESAUCE
CRACKER PUDDING*
BLACK WALNUT CAKE*   COFFEE

Dinner V

PENNSYLVANIA DUTCH MEAT LOAF*
FRIED SWEET POTATOES   STUFFED CABBAGE*
BUTTERED PEAS   DRIED CORN*
APPLESAUCE
LETTUCE AND ONION SALAD*
CELERY   PICKLES   OLIVES
RYE BREAD*   WHITE BREAD*
JELLY AND JAM
BEAN PICKLE*   PICKLED BEETS*
PICKLED WATERMELON*   SPICED PEACHES*
LEMON CAKE PIE*   COFFEE   TEA

Supper 1

BROWN FLOUR POTATO SOUP*
APPLESAUCE
RED BEET EGGS*   PICKLES   CELERY HEARTS
BREAD AND BUTTER   APPLE BUTTER*
EGG CHEESE*
SLICED DRIED BEEF   CRACKERS
SHOO-FLY PIE*   SPEARMINT TEA

Supper II

CHICKEN CORN SOUP*
RAISED POTATO CAKES*
PEPPER CABBAGE*   RED BEET EGGS*
HOME-CANNED FRUIT
QUAKERTOWN PIE*

Supper III

LEBANON BOLOGNA   SOUSE*
POTATO BALLS*
DRIED CORN*   SLICED TOMATOES
TURNIP SLAW*
BREAD AND BUTTER
BAKED TAPIOCA*   MORAVIAN SUGAR CAKE*

Where to Get It

Pennsylvania Dutch food products are available by mail for those who live outside of the Pennsylvania Dutch area. The following sources of the various items are recommended:

Dried Corn
   John Cope Corn Co.
   East Petersburg
   Pennsylvania

Saffron and Dried Apple Schnitz
   Shenk's Extracts
   Neffsville
   Pennsylvania
      17556

Cup Cheese
    C. H. Shenk Cheese House
    R.D. 6
    Lancaster
    Pennsylvania

Lebanon Bologna
    Seltzer's Bologna
    Palmyra
    Pennsylvania

Pennsylvania Dutch Pretzels
    Sturgis Pretzel House
    Lititz
    Pennsylvania

Sweets and Sours

    (1.)
    Spring Glen Farm Kitchen
    R.D. 3
    Ephrata
    Pennsylvania
        (Write for folder)

    (2.)
    Kresge Farm Products
    Lehighton
    Pennsylvania
        (Write for folder)

Sources of References

All of the recipes in THE ART OF PENNSYLVANIA DUTCH COOKING have been acquired through personal contacts over the past thirty years. Not only have I had the good fortune of a Pennsylvania Dutch heritage, but, I have known many generous cooks who gladly told me how they (or their mothers or grandmothers) made "so-and-so." For comparison of recipes, and to check their Pennsylvania Dutch authenticity, the following books have been used for reference.

BOOKS

American Heritage Publishing Co., *The American Heritage Cookbook* (New York: Simon and Schuster, Inc., 1964) 630 pages

Frederick, J. George, *The Pennsylvania Dutch and Their Cookery* (New York: The Business Bourse, 1935) 275 pages

Hark, Ann, *Hex Marks the Spot* (New York: J. B. Lippincott Co., 1938) 316 pages

Hark, Ann, *Blue Hills and Shoo-Fly Pie* (New York: J. B. Lippincott Co., 1952) 284 pages

Hark, Ann, and Barba, Preston, *Pennsylvania German Cookery* (Allentown, Pennsylvania: Schlechters, 1950) 258 pages

Hutchison, Ruth, *The Pennsylvania Dutch Cookbook* (New York: Harper and Brothers, 1948) 213 pages

Shoemaker, Alfred L., *Christmas in Pennsylvania* (Kutztown, Pennsylvania: Pennsylvania Folklife Society, 1959) 116 pages

Shoemaker, Alfred L., *Eastertide in Pennsylvania* (Kutztown, Pennsylvania: Pennsylvania Folklife Society, 1960) 96 pages

Showalter, Mary Emma, *Mennonite Community Cookbook* (Scottdale, Pennsylvania: Mennonite Community Association, 1950) 494 pages

Sisters of the Brethren Church, *The Inglenook Cook Book* (Elgin, Illinois: Brethren Publishing House, 1909) 212 pages

The Browns, Cora, Rose, and Bob, *America Cooks* (Garden City, New York: Doubleday and Co., 1940) 986 pages

BOOKLETS

Appel, *Pennsylvania Dutch Recipes* (Lancaster, Pennsylvania)

Aurand, A. Monroe, Jr., *Cooking with the Pennsylvania "Dutch"* (Harrisburg: The Aurand Press, 1946) 32 pages

Auxiliary Members of Jefferson Volunteer Fire Co., *Jefferson's Favorite Recipes* (Codorus, Pennsylvania)

Barbara Snyder Sunday School Class of Moravian Church, *Lititz Springs Cook Book* (Lititz, Pennsylvania) 42 pages

Berks County Federation of Women's Clubs, *Cookbook of Pennsylvania Dutch Recipes*

Culinary Arts Press, *Pennsylvania Dutch Cook Book of Fine Old Recipes* (Reading, Pennsylvania, 1936) 48 pages

Davidow, Leonard S., *Pennsylvania Dutch Cookbook of Fine Old Recipes* (Reading, Pennsylvania, 1934) 48 pages

Gardner, Margaret Knoll, *Best Loved Pennsylvania Dutch Recipes* (Lancaster, Pennsylvania, 1963) 28 pages

Healy, Dorothy W., *Typical Pennsylvania Recipes* (Allentown, Pennsylvania: Bethlehem Gas Co., 1950) 73 pages

Lancaster County Federation of Women's Clubs, *Our Kitchen Favorites*

Ladies' Bible Class of the Jerusalem Lutheran Sunday School, *Kum Essa* (Rothsville, Pennsylvania, 1950) 75 pages

Lutheran Women's Guild of Messiah Evangelical Lutheran Church, *Downingtown's Own Cookbook* (Downingtown, Pennsylvania) 44 pages

Members of Lutheran Church Choir, *Recipes Tried and True* (Downingtown, Pennsylvania: Downingtown Publishing Co. 1909) 200 pages

Pennsylvania Future Homemakers of America, *The PFHA Cookbook of Teenagers' Favorite Recipes* (Harrisburg: Department of Public Instruction) 143 pages

Society of Farm Women, *Garden Spot Recipes* (Mt. Joy, Pennsylvania: The Bulletin Press 1931) 75 pages

Robacker, Earl F., *Pennsylvania German Cooky Cutters and Cookies* (Plymouth Meeting, Pennsylvania) 40 pages

The Gleaners' S. S. Class, Fishburn's Evangelical U. B. Church, *A Scoop of This. . . . . A Pinch of That!* (Hershey, Pennsylvania, 1959) 104 pages

Wieand, Paul R., *Folk Medicine Plants* (Allentown, Pennsylvania: Wieand's Pennsylvania Dutch, 1961) 48 pages

Willing Workers Class of Calvary Methodist Church, *Stewartstown Cookbook* (Stewartstown, Pennsylvania) 104 pages

Women's Guild of Zion's Church, *Cookbook* (Windsor Castle, Pennsylvania, 1951) 4th ed., 98 pages

Yorkraft, Inc., *Pennsylvania Dutch Recipes* (York, Pennsylvania: Yorkraft, 1960) 48 pages

Index